Highlights of women's earnings in 2013

In 2013, women who were full-time wage and salary workers had median usual weekly earnings of $706. On average in 2013, women made 82 percent of the median weekly earnings of male full-time wage and salary workers ($860). In 1979, the first year for which comparable earnings data are available, women earned 62 percent of what men earned. (See chart 1 and tables 1 and 12.)

This report presents earnings data from the Current Population Survey (CPS), a national monthly survey of approximately 60,000 households conducted by the U.S. Census Bureau for the U.S. Bureau of Labor Statistics (BLS). Information on earnings is collected from one-fourth of the CPS sample each month. It is important to

note that the comparisons of earnings in this report are on a broad level and do not control for many factors that can be significant in explaining earnings differences. See the accompanying technical notes section for more information, including a description of the source of the data and an explanation of the concepts and definitions used in this report.

Earnings of full-time workers

Below are data highlights for women and men who work full time, with sections focusing on characteristics such as age, race and ethnicity, education, occupation, and more.

Age

Median weekly earnings were highest for women age 35 to 64 in 2013, with little difference in the earnings of 35- to 44-year-olds ($767), 45- to 54-year-olds ($761), and 55- to 64-year-olds ($779). Among men, workers who were age

CONTENTS

Chart 1

Women's earnings as a percentage of men's, for full-time wage and salary workers, 1979–2013 annual averages

In percent

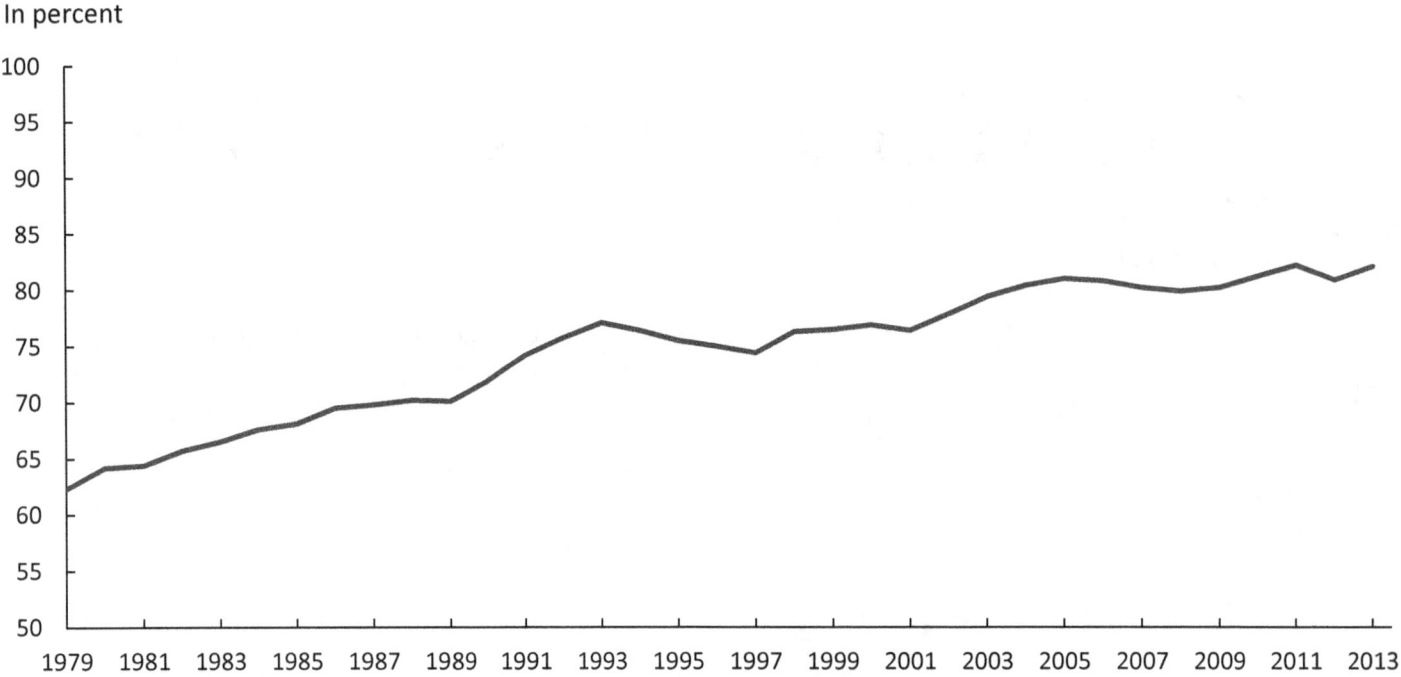

Note: Percentages are calculated from annual averages of median usual weekly earnings for full-time wage and salary workers.
Source: U.S. Bureau of Labor Statistics.

45 to 64 had the highest earnings, with 45- to 54-year-olds ($994) making about the same as 55- to 64-year-olds ($1,011). Young women and men age 16 to 24 had the lowest earnings ($423 and $479, respectively). (See table 1.)

Among the four age groupings of those 35 years and older, women's earnings ranged from 74 percent to 80 percent of the earnings of their male counterparts. In the younger age groups, the earnings differences between women and men were smaller, with women earning 89 to 90 percent of what men earned. (See table 1.)

Between 1979 and 2013, women's-to-men's earnings ratios rose for most age groups. Among 25- to 34-year-olds, for example, the ratio increased from 68 percent in 1979 to 89 percent in 2013, while the ratio for 45- to 54-year-olds increased from 57 percent to 77 percent. (See table 12.)

Race and ethnicity

Asian women and men earned more than their White, Black, and Hispanic or Latino counterparts in 2013.

Among women, Whites ($722) earned 88 percent as much as Asian women ($819), while Blacks ($606) and Hispanics ($541) earned 74 percent and 66 percent as much as their Asian counterparts, respectively. In comparison, White men ($884) earned 83 percent as much as Asian men ($1,059); Black men ($664) earned 63 percent as much; and Hispanic men ($594), 56 percent. (See chart 2 and table 1.)

Earnings differences between women and men were the most pronounced for Asians and for Whites. Asian women earned 77 percent as much as Asian men in 2013, and White women earned 82 percent as much as their male counterparts. In comparison, Black and Hispanic women had median earnings that were 91 percent of those of their male counterparts. (See table 1.)

When adjusted for inflation, women's earnings since 1979 have increased considerably across the major race and Hispanic ethnicity categories. Earnings growth has been greatest for White women, outpacing that of their Black

Chart 2

Median usual weekly earnings of women and men who are full-time wage and salary workers, by race and Hispanic or Latino ethnicity, 2013 annual averages

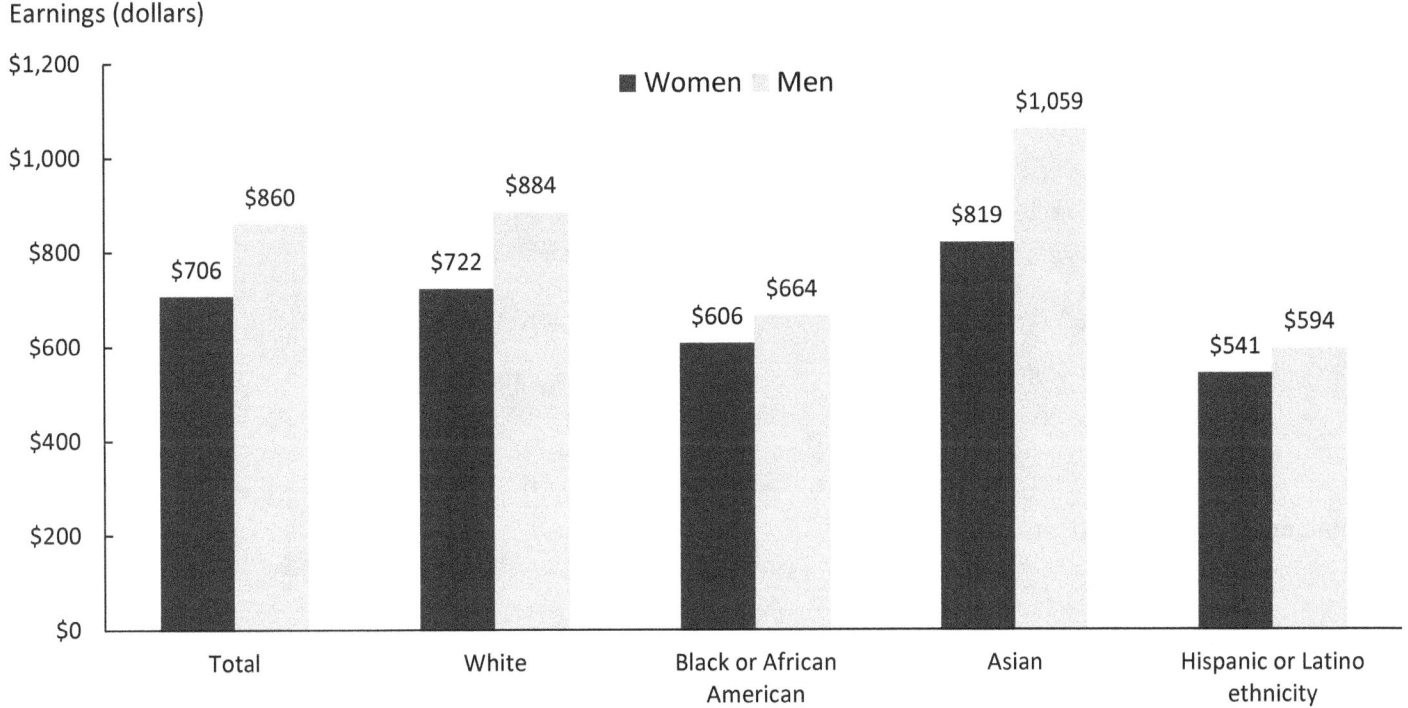

Earnings (dollars)

Note: People of Hispanic or Latino ethnicity may be of any race. Estimates for the race groups shown (White, Black or African American, and Asian) include Hispanics.

Source: U.S. Bureau of Labor Statistics.

and Hispanic counterparts. Between 1979 and 2013, inflation-adjusted earnings (also called constant-dollar earnings) rose by 31 percent for White women, compared with an increase of 20 percent for Black women and 15 percent for Hispanic women. In contrast, inflation-adjusted earnings for White and Black men declined slightly (1 percent and 2 percent, respectively) from 1979 to 2013, and Hispanic men's earnings fell by 9 percent. (See table 18.) Asians were not included in this analysis because comparable data for the group are not available until 2003. (See note in table 18.)

Education

Median weekly earnings vary significantly by level of educational attainment. Among all workers age 25 and older, the weekly earnings of those without a high school diploma ($472) were two-fifths of those with a bachelor's degree or higher ($1,194) in 2013. For workers with a

high school diploma who had not attended college ($651), median earnings were a little more than half of those with a bachelor's degree or higher. Earnings for those with some college or an associate's degree ($748) were just under two-thirds of what workers with a bachelor's degree or more made. (See table 1.)

At each level of education, women have fared better than men with respect to earnings growth. Although both women and men without a high school diploma have experienced declines in inflation-adjusted earnings since 1979, the drop for women was much smaller than that for men: a 12-percent decrease for women as opposed to a 34-percent decline for men. On an inflation-adjusted basis, earnings for women with a bachelor's degree or higher have increased by 32 percent since 1979, while those of their male counterparts have risen by 18 percent. (Data pertain to workers age 25 and older.) (See chart 3 and table 19.)

Chart 3

Percentage change in inflation-adjusted median usual weekly earnings of women and men, by educational attainment, 1979–2013

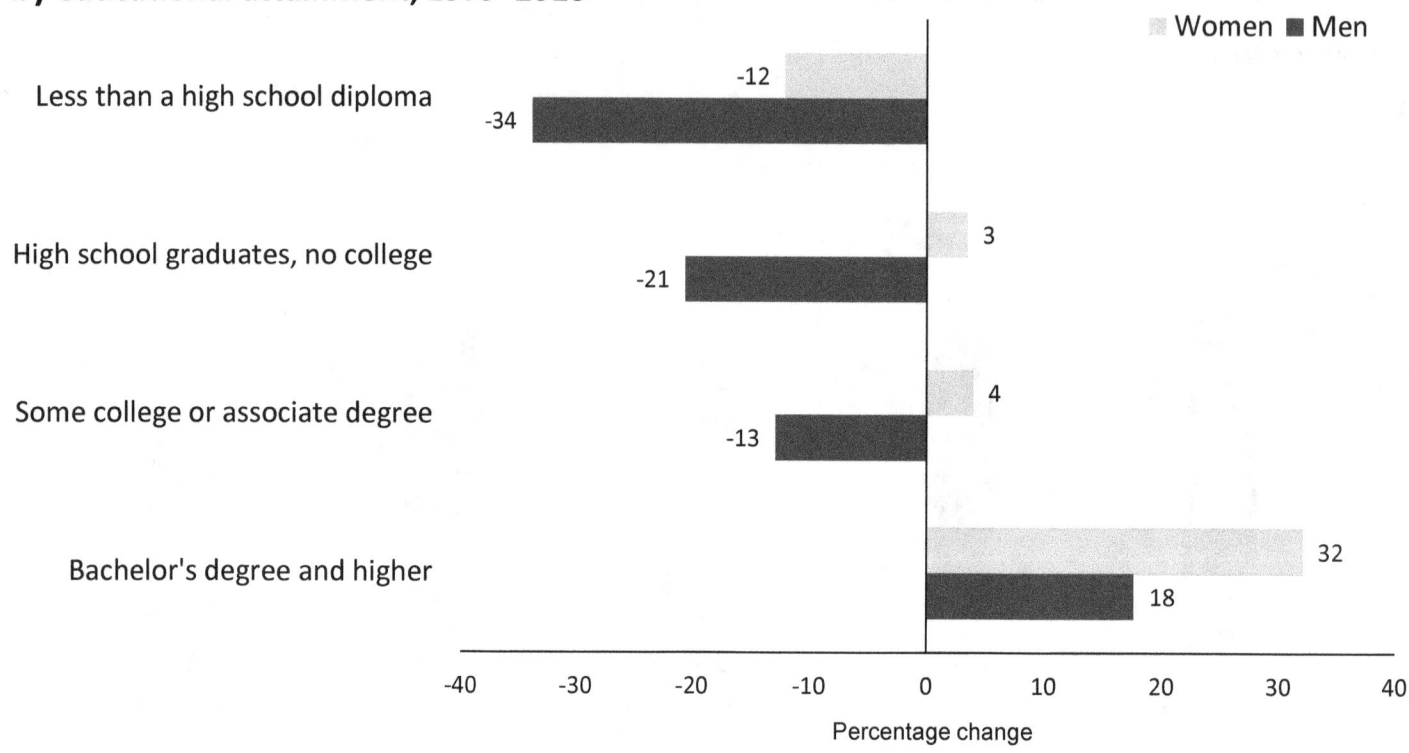

Note: Data relate to earnings of full-time wage and salary workers, 25 years and older.
Source: U.S. Bureau of Labor Statistics.

Occupation

Among both women and men, median weekly earnings for those working full time in management, business, and financial operations jobs were higher than in any other major occupational category in 2013 ($1,049 for women and $1,412 for men). Of women in management, business, and financial operations occupations, those who were chief executives and computer and information systems managers had the highest median weekly earnings ($1,811 and $1,549, respectively). Among men in this job group, chief executives and architectural and engineering managers had the highest earnings ($2,266 and $1,898, respectively). The second highest paying major occupational category for women and men was professional and related occupations ($944 for women and $1,295 for men). Among women in professional and related occupations, those who were pharmacists ($1,802) and lawyers ($1,566) had the highest earnings. For men in professional and related

occupations, those who were pharmacists ($2,092), physicians and surgeons ($2,087), and lawyers ($1,986) earned the most. (See table 2.)

The occupational distributions of female and male full-time workers differ considerably. Compared with men, relatively few women work in construction, production, or transportation occupations, and women are far more concentrated in office and administrative support jobs. (See table 2.)

Women are more likely than men to work in professional and related occupations. In 2013, 29 percent of women worked in professional and related occupations, compared with 19 percent of men. Within this occupational category, though, the proportion of women employed in the higher paying job groups is much smaller than the proportion of men employed in them. In 2013, 9 percent of women in professional and related occupations were employed in the relatively high-paying computer and

Chart 4

Distribution of full-time wage and salary employment for women and men, by major occupational group, 2013 annual averages

Percentage of total employment

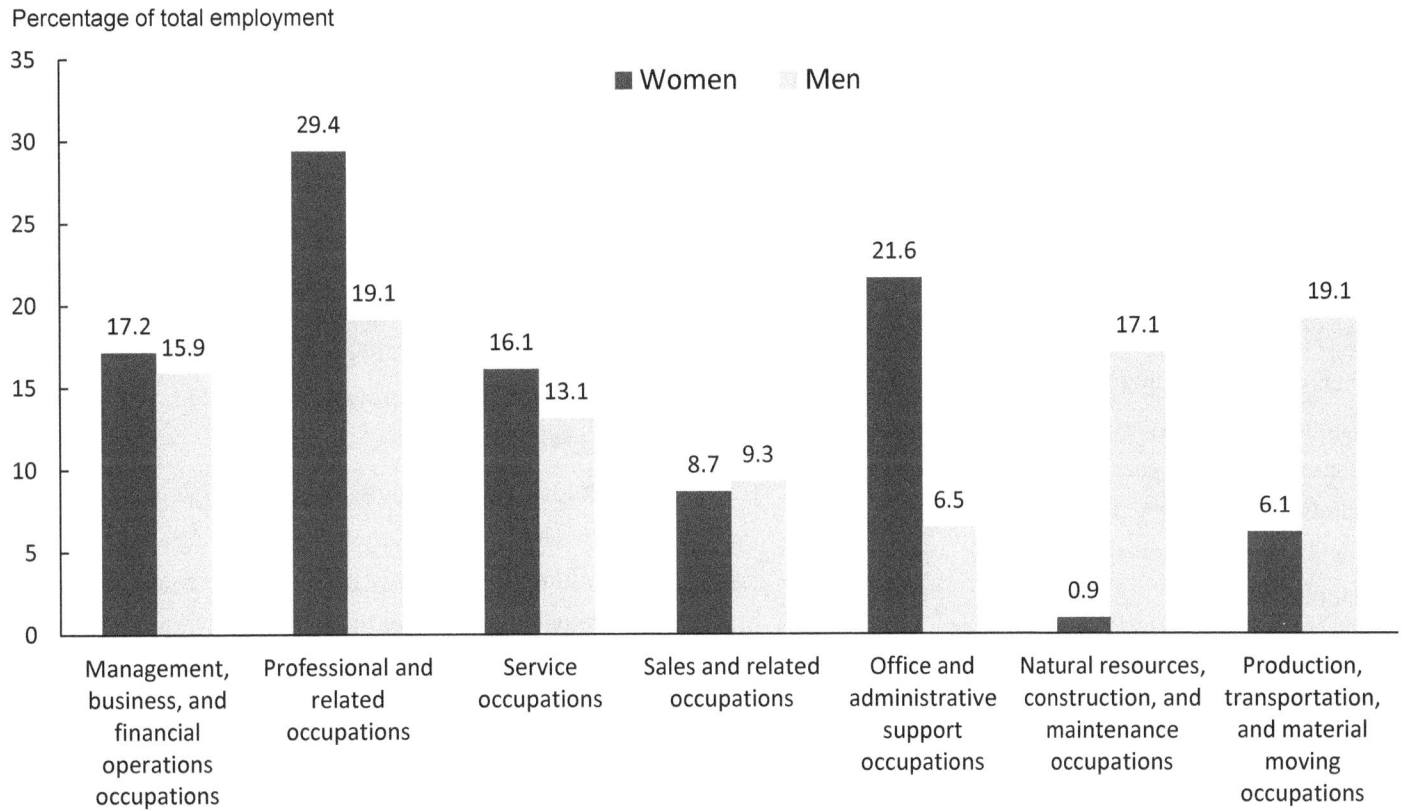

Source: U.S. Bureau of Labor Statistics.

engineering fields, compared with 44 percent of men. Women in professional and related occupations were more likely to work in education and healthcare jobs, in which the pay is generally lower than that for computer and engineering jobs. Sixty-nine percent of women in professional occupations worked in education and healthcare jobs in 2013, compared with 30 percent of men. (See chart 4 and table 2.)

Earnings among parents

In 2013, a little more than one-third of full-time wage and salary workers were parents of children under age 18 (36 percent of women and 37 percent of men). Among women, median weekly earnings for mothers of children under age 18 ($701) were essentially the same as earnings for women without children under 18 ($708). Among men, earnings for fathers with children under 18 were $950, compared with $804 for men without children under 18. (See table 7.)

State of residence

Median weekly earnings and women's-to-men's earnings ratios vary by state of residence. (In this section, "state" refers to the 50 states and the District of Columbia.) The differences among the states reflect, in part, variation in the occupations and industries found in each state and differences in the demographic composition of each state's labor force. In general, the sampling error for the state estimates is considerably larger than it is for the national estimates; thus, comparisons of state estimates should be made with caution. In addition, it should be noted that while earnings are shown based on workers' state of residence, their reported earnings may or may not be from a job located in the same state. (See table 3.)

Weekly work hours

Among full-time workers (that is, those working at a job 35 hours or more per week), men are more likely than women to have a longer workweek. Twenty-five percent of men worked 41 or more hours per week in 2013, compared with 14 percent of women who did so. Women were more likely than men to work 35 to 39 hours per week: 12 percent of women worked those hours in 2013, while 5 percent of men did. A large majority of both male and female full-time workers had a 40-hour workweek; among these workers, women earned 90 percent as much as men earned. (People who usually work 35 or more hours per week but whose hours vary were excluded from this analysis.) (See table 5.)

Earnings of part-time workers

Women are more likely than men to work part time—that is, less than 35 hours per week on a sole or principal job. Women who worked part time made up 26 percent of all female wage and salary workers in 2013. In contrast, 13 percent of men in wage and salary jobs worked part time. (See tables 4 and 5.)

Women and men who worked part time had fairly similar median earnings. Median weekly earnings for female part-timers were $241 in 2013, slightly above the $230 median for their male counterparts. (See table 4.)

Men who work part time tend to be younger than women who work part time. In 2013, 43 percent of male part-time workers were 16 to 24 years old, compared with 29 percent of female part-time workers. (See table 4.)

Earnings of workers paid by the hour

Sixty-two percent of women and 56 percent of men employed in wage and salary jobs were paid by the hour in 2013. Women who were paid hourly rates had median hourly earnings of $12.12, which was 87 percent of the median for men paid by the hour ($14.00). (See tables 8 and 11.)

Among workers who were paid hourly rates in 2013, 5 percent of women and 3 percent of men had hourly earnings at or below the prevailing federal minimum wage of $7.25. (See table 10.)

Among both women and men, hourly paid workers age 16 to 19 were the most likely to have earnings at or below the minimum wage. Twenty percent of teenage workers who were paid hourly rates earned the prevailing federal minimum wage or less in 2013, compared with just 3 percent of hourly paid workers age 25 and older. Eight percent of workers age 20 to 24 had earnings at or below the minimum wage. (See table 10.) See the technical notes section for information about estimating the number of minimum wage workers.

Statistical Tables

Table 1. Median usual weekly earnings of full-time wage and salary workers, by selected characteristics, 2013 annual averages

Characteristic	Total			Women			Men			Women's earnings as a percent-age of men's
	Number of workers (in thousands)	Median weekly earnings	Standard error of median	Number of workers (in thousands)	Median weekly earnings	Standard error of median	Number of workers (in thousands)	Median weekly earnings	Standard error of median	
Age										
Total, 16 years and older....................	104,262	$776	$2	46,268	$706	$3	57,994	$860	$3	82.1
16 to 24 years..............................	9,247	454	4	4,041	423	3	5,207	479	4	88.3
16 to 19 years..........................	1,084	373	5	453	350	7	630	390	6	89.7
20 to 24 years..........................	8,164	472	4	3,587	442	5	4,577	492	4	89.8
25 years and older.........................	95,015	827	2	42,228	740	2	52,787	912	3	81.1
25 to 34 years..........................	25,081	708	4	10,891	665	4	14,190	744	5	89.4
35 to 44 years..........................	24,303	874	5	10,480	767	5	13,823	956	7	80.2
45 to 54 years..........................	25,100	883	4	11,391	761	5	13,708	994	7	76.6
55 to 64 years..........................	17,066	904	5	7,967	779	7	9,100	1,011	9	77.1
65 years and older......................	3,465	801	16	1,498	691	13	1,966	937	19	73.7
Race and Hispanic or Latino Ethnicity										
White..	82,672	802	3	35,619	722	3	47,053	884	3	81.7
Black or African American....................	12,439	629	4	6,588	606	4	5,851	664	7	91.3
Asian..	6,073	942	11	2,698	819	17	3,376	1,059	21	77.3
Hispanic or Latino ethnicity..................	16,859	578	4	6,534	541	7	10,325	594	4	91.1
Marital Status										
Never married.................................	28,410	613	2	12,594	597	3	15,817	627	4	95.2
Married, spouse present......................	58,610	894	3	23,915	768	3	34,695	985	5	78.0
Other marital status..........................	17,242	740	4	9,760	692	6	7,483	814	8	85.0
Divorced....................................	11,568	779	6	6,548	730	6	5,020	870	10	83.9
Separated..................................	4,092	637	10	2,031	596	8	2,061	701	12	85.0
Widowed...................................	1,582	696	12	1,181	671	16	401	774	40	86.7
Union Affiliation[1]										
Members of unions[2]..........................	13,020	950	5	5,612	898	7	7,409	991	7	90.6
Represented by unions[3]......................	14,341	944	5	6,248	893	7	8,093	985	7	90.7
Not represented by a union..................	89,921	750	2	40,020	676	3	49,902	831	4	81.3
Educational Attainment										
Total, 25 years and older.....................	95,015	827	2	42,228	740	2	52,787	912	3	81.1
Less than a high school diploma..........	6,956	472	4	2,133	400	4	4,822	500	3	80.0
High school graduates, no college........	25,043	651	3	10,115	573	3	14,928	732	4	78.3
Some college or associate degree........	26,034	748	3	12,346	657	4	13,688	858	6	76.6
Bachelor's degree and higher..............	36,982	1,194	7	17,633	1,043	5	19,349	1,395	8	74.8

[1] Differences in earnings levels between workers with and without union affiliation reflect a variety of factors in addition to coverage by a collective bargaining agreement, including the distribution of workers by occupation, industry, and geographic region.

[2] Data refer to members of a labor union or an employee association similar to a union.

[3] Data refer to both union members and workers who report no union affiliation but whose jobs are covered by a union or an employee association contract.

Note: Estimates for the race groups shown (White, Black or African American, and Asian) do not sum to totals because data are not presented for all race groups. People of Hispanic or Latino ethnicity may be of any race; estimates for the race groups include Hispanics.
Source: U.S. Bureau of Labor Statistics.

Table 2. Median usual weekly earnings of full-time wage and salary workers, by detailed occupation, 2013 annual averages
[Numbers in thousands]

Occupation	Total			Women			Men			Women's earnings as a percentage of men's
	Number of workers	Median weekly earnings	Standard error of median	Number of workers	Median weekly earnings	Standard error of median	Number of workers	Median weekly earnings	Standard error of median	
Total, full-time wage and salary workers....	104,262	$776	$2	46,268	$706	$3	57,994	$860	$3	82.1
Management, professional, and related occupations.................................	41,820	1,132	4	21,530	973	4	20,290	1,349	6	72.1
Management, business, and financial operations occupations...................	17,137	1,208	10	7,937	1,049	8	9,200	1,412	12	74.3
Management occupations...............	11,501	1,285	16	4,737	1,103	16	6,764	1,456	12	75.8
Chief executives.......................	1,051	2,069	72	286	1,811	107	764	2,266	98	79.9
General and operations managers...	947	1,370	32	250	1,161	43	698	1,444	33	80.4
Legislators..............................	10	–	–	4	–	–	6	–	–	–
Advertising and promotions managers...........................	53	1,526	590	35	–	–	18	–	–	–
Marketing and sales managers.......	829	1,389	41	353	1,124	39	476	1,658	34	67.8
Public relations and fundraising managers...........................	51	1,159	27	29	–	–	21	–	–	–
Administrative services managers. ..	109	1,198	76	38	–	–	71	1,232	70	–
Computer and information systems managers...........................	570	1,728	51	163	1,549	54	407	1,769	98	87.6
Financial managers...................	1,127	1,236	22	613	1,064	24	514	1,518	43	70.1
Compensation and benefits managers...........................	11	–	–	8	–	–	3	–	–	–
Human resources managers.........	211	1,327	169	152	1,240	49	60	1,536	67	80.7
Training and development managers...........................	33	–	–	17	–	–	16	–	–	–
Industrial production managers.......	256	1,338	39	41	–	–	215	1,352	44	–
Purchasing managers.................	181	1,358	52	89	1,290	63	92	1,441	22	89.5
Transportation, storage, and distribution managers..............	252	1,005	26	58	920	124	194	1,029	49	89.4
Farmers, ranchers, and other agricultural managers..............	97	731	37	19	–	–	78	716	68	–
Construction managers...............	414	1,275	63	38	–	–	376	1,328	54	–
Education administrators..............	698	1,259	23	450	1,130	33	248	1,543	40	73.2
Architectural and engineering managers...........................	117	1,894	24	13	–	–	104	1,898	25	–
Food service managers..............	716	701	19	335	620	12	381	801	45	77.4
Funeral service managers............	4	–	–	3	–	–	1	–	–	–
Gaming managers.....................	16	–	–	4	–	–	12	–	–	–
Lodging managers.....................	98	901	48	53	858	152	45	–	–	–
Medical and health services managers...........................	529	1,258	30	375	1,224	34	154	1,412	91	86.7
Natural sciences managers...........	12	–	–	4	–	–	8	–	–	–
Postmasters and mail superintendents....................	30	–	–	17	–	–	13	–	–	–
Property, real estate, and community association managers...........................	358	862	39	198	784	30	161	1,068	100	73.4
Social and community service managers...........................	280	1,042	50	185	1,004	61	94	1,150	58	87.3
Emergency management directors...	9	–	–	3	–	–	6	–	–	–
Managers, all other...................	2,431	1,264	22	905	1,105	31	1,527	1,399	36	79.0
Business and financial operations occupations...........................	5,636	1,091	14	3,199	979	13	2,436	1,263	21	77.5
Agents and business managers of artists, performers, and athletes. ..	38	–	–	18	–	–	20	–	–	–
Buyers and purchasing agents, farm products.............................	17	–	–	5	–	–	11	–	–	–

Table 2. Median usual weekly earnings of full-time wage and salary workers, by detailed occupation, 2013 annual averages — Continued
[Numbers in thousands]

Occupation	Total			Women			Men			Women's earnings as a percent-age of men's
	Number of workers	Median weekly earnings	Standard error of median	Number of workers	Median weekly earnings	Standard error of median	Number of workers	Median weekly earnings	Standard error of median	
Wholesale and retail buyers, except farm products........................	158	899	31	88	930	49	71	871	37	106.8
Purchasing agents, except wholesale, retail, and farm products...............................	263	984	28	151	912	26	112	1,116	71	81.7
Claims adjusters, appraisers, examiners, and investigators.......	300	931	32	195	838	41	104	1,144	29	73.3
Compliance officers.....................	182	1,124	53	99	1,081	58	83	1,170	94	92.4
Cost estimators..........................	102	1,050	52	13	–	–	89	1,071	52	–
Human resources workers............	498	981	34	366	958	22	131	1,139	50	84.1
Compensation, benefits, and job analysis specialists..................	72	1,033	89	59	1,010	99	14	–	–	–
Training and development specialists.............................	109	1,079	68	62	979	277	47	–	–	–
Logisticians..............................	91	993	40	33	–	–	58	1,045	154	–
Management analysts.................	547	1,450	35	229	1,319	101	318	1,614	65	81.7
Meeting, convention, and event planners...............................	95	930	56	80	901	119	15	–	–	–
Fundraisers..............................	80	1,124	89	58	1,084	133	22	–	–	–
Market research analysts and marketing specialists...............	190	1,139	36	110	967	39	80	1,171	57	82.6
Business operations specialists, all other.................................	180	1,044	28	110	899	66	69	1,226	70	73.3
Accountants and auditors............	1,516	1,109	23	945	1,029	24	571	1,268	55	81.2
Appraisers and assessors of real estate..................................	60	1,142	91	27	–	–	33	–	–	–
Budget analysts........................	58	1,389	93	26	–	–	31	–	–	–
Credit analysts.........................	31	–	–	19	–	–	12	–	–	–
Financial analysts.....................	89	1,466	87	33	–	–	56	1,757	94	–
Personal financial advisors...........	288	1,424	105	72	1,149	52	215	1,565	56	73.4
Insurance underwriters...............	98	1,045	110	61	879	57	37	–	–	–
Financial examiners...................	10	–	–	6	–	–	4	–	–	–
Credit counselors and loan officers...	360	970	35	208	864	33	152	1,162	68	74.4
Tax examiners and collectors, and revenue agents....................	62	952	25	43	–	–	19	–	–	–
Tax preparers...........................	56	767	33	34	–	–	22	–	–	–
Financial specialists, all other........	87	962	50	49	–	–	38	–	–	–
Professional and related occupations.....	24,683	1,071	6	13,594	944	5	11,089	1,295	14	72.9
Computer and mathematical occupations............................	3,621	1,365	14	928	1,174	20	2,693	1,452	18	80.9
Computer and information research scientists.............................	15	–	–	3	–	–	12	–	–	–
Computer systems analysts...........	443	1,367	32	158	1,216	75	285	1,455	33	83.6
Information security analysts.........	53	1,460	248	10	–	–	43	–	–	–
Computer programmers..............	437	1,372	36	106	1,162	58	332	1,428	51	81.4
Software developers, applications and systems software..............	1,053	1,643	26	209	1,370	40	844	1,737	18	78.9
Web developers........................	137	1,060	97	53	937	153	84	1,157	59	81.0
Computer support specialists.........	474	980	28	134	901	74	340	1,019	37	88.4
Database administrators..............	95	1,345	71	30	–	–	65	1,563	160	–
Network and computer systems administrators.......................	210	1,237	34	37	–	–	173	1,252	34	–
Computer network architects........	131	1,630	93	9	–	–	122	1,593	132	–
Computer occupations, all other......	359	1,149	31	81	1,176	52	277	1,136	42	103.5
Actuaries................................	25	–	–	9	–	–	17	–	–	–
Mathematicians........................	2	–	–	0	–	–	2	–	–	–

Table 2. Median usual weekly earnings of full-time wage and salary workers, by detailed occupation, 2013 annual averages — Continued
[Numbers in thousands]

Occupation	Total			Women			Men			Women's earnings as a percent-age of men's
	Number of workers	Median weekly earnings	Standard error of median	Number of workers	Median weekly earnings	Standard error of median	Number of workers	Median weekly earnings	Standard error of median	
Operations research analysts.........	119	1,444	45	63	1,313	105	56	1,569	95	83.7
Statisticians.............................	65	1,414	87	23	–	–	42	–	–	–
Miscellaneous mathematical science occupations...........................	1	–	–	1	–	–	0	–	–	–
Architecture and engineering occupations...........................	2,540	1,365	13	330	1,143	27	2,209	1,403	22	81.5
Architects, except naval...............	118	1,292	55	30	–	–	88	1,347	37	–
Surveyors, cartographers, and photogrammetrists..................	32	–	–	9	–	–	22	–	–	–
Aerospace engineers..................	137	1,865	87	13	–	–	124	1,873	72	–
Agricultural engineers.................	3	–	–	0	–	–	3	–	–	–
Biomedical engineers.................	10	–	–	2	–	–	9	–	–	–
Chemical engineers...................	56	1,568	431	8	–	–	48	–	–	–
Civil engineers.........................	324	1,373	35	36	–	–	288	1,417	53	–
Computer hardware engineers.......	92	1,507	69	10	–	–	82	1,544	41	–
Electrical and electronics engineers.............................	268	1,522	49	21	–	–	247	1,514	58	–
Environmental engineers..............	28	–	–	6	–	–	22	–	–	–
Industrial engineers, including health and safety...........................	181	1,385	71	30	–	–	151	1,417	56	–
Marine engineers and naval architects.............................	12	–	–	0	–	–	12	–	–	–
Materials engineers....................	43	–	–	7	–	–	36	–	–	–
Mechanical engineers..................	297	1,496	94	24	–	–	273	1,554	63	–
Mining and geological engineers, including mining safety engineers...........................	16	–	–	2	–	–	13	–	–	–
Nuclear engineers......................	4	–	–	0	–	–	4	–	–	–
Petroleum engineers...................	34	–	–	2	–	–	33	–	–	–
Engineers, all other...................	371	1,528	37	48	–	–	322	1,561	37	–
Drafters.................................	104	974	53	20	–	–	85	991	30	–
Engineering technicians, except drafters...............................	361	1,011	24	59	934	92	302	1,027	33	90.9
Surveying and mapping technicians...........................	48	–	–	5	–	–	43	–	–	–
Life, physical, and social science occupations...........................	1,063	1,152	16	456	1,030	32	608	1,271	66	81.0
Agricultural and food scientists.......	30	–	–	12	–	–	19	–	–	–
Biological scientists....................	107	1,157	49	53	1,104	109	54	1,233	153	89.5
Conservation scientists and foresters.............................	27	–	–	5	–	–	23	–	–	–
Medical scientists......................	131	1,216	160	73	1,142	57	58	1,430	346	79.9
Life scientists, all other...............	1	–	–	0	–	–	1	–	–	–
Astronomers and physicists..........	13	–	–	1	–	–	13	–	–	–
Atmospheric and space scientists....	11	–	–	2	–	–	9	–	–	–
Chemists and materials scientists....	109	1,182	87	42	–	–	68	1,380	72	–
Environmental scientists and geoscientists........................	76	1,330	201	18	–	–	58	1,392	77	–
Physical scientists, all other...........	132	1,517	62	44	–	–	88	1,597	58	–
Economists.............................	29	–	–	14	–	–	15	–	–	–
Survey researchers....................	1	–	–	1	–	–	0	–	–	–
Psychologists..........................	96	1,267	153	69	1,178	97	27	–	–	–
Sociologists............................	4	–	–	3	–	–	2	–	–	–
Urban and regional planners..........	20	–	–	7	–	–	12	–	–	–
Miscellaneous social scientists and related workers......................	40	–	–	18	–	–	22	–	–	–

Table 2. Median usual weekly earnings of full-time wage and salary workers, by detailed occupation, 2013 annual averages — Continued
[Numbers in thousands]

Occupation	Total			Women			Men			Women's earnings as a percentage of men's
	Number of workers	Median weekly earnings	Standard error of median	Number of workers	Median weekly earnings	Standard error of median	Number of workers	Median weekly earnings	Standard error of median	
Agricultural and food science technicians.............................	23	–	–	12	–	–	12	–	–	–
Biological technicians..................	16	–	–	8	–	–	9	–	–	–
Chemical technicians...................	62	849	61	21	–	–	41	–	–	–
Geological and petroleum technicians.............................	23	–	–	5	–	–	18	–	–	–
Nuclear technicians....................	1	–	–	1	–	–	0	–	–	–
Social science research assistants...	2	–	–	1	–	–	2	–	–	–
Miscellaneous life, physical, and social science technicians..........	105	761	29	47	–	–	59	911	134	–
Community and social service occupations.............................	1,913	847	14	1,158	808	12	755	930	23	86.9
Counselors.............................	568	885	26	391	884	27	178	889	63	99.4
Social workers.........................	636	845	23	507	818	15	129	978	60	83.6
Probation officers and correctional treatment specialists...............	105	888	53	43	–	–	62	927	46	–
Social and human service assistants.............................	102	668	43	68	641	39	34	–	–	–
Miscellaneous community and social service specialists, including health educators and community health workers........................	83	756	38	64	740	32	19	–	–	–
Clergy.................................	343	935	26	47	–	–	296	968	35	–
Directors, religious activities and education.............................	41	–	–	21	–	–	20	–	–	–
Religious workers, all other...........	34	–	–	17	–	–	17	–	–	–
Legal occupations........................	1,305	1,253	22	707	1,010	23	598	1,764	69	57.3
Lawyers................................	710	1,880	36	247	1,566	51	463	1,986	103	78.9
Judicial law clerks.....................	9	–	–	6	–	–	3	–	–	–
Judges, magistrates, and other judicial workers......................	49	–	–	19	–	–	30	–	–	–
Paralegals and legal assistants.......	337	846	31	287	825	29	50	923	50	89.4
Miscellaneous legal support workers...............................	199	873	44	148	787	67	51	1,013	289	77.7
Education, training, and library occupations.............................	6,589	937	6	4,782	888	7	1,808	1,091	26	81.4
Postsecondary teachers...............	893	1,172	27	424	1,100	37	469	1,338	36	82.2
Preschool and kindergarten teachers...............................	496	638	41	484	624	31	12	–	–	–
Elementary and middle school teachers...............................	2,669	954	9	2,138	937	10	531	1,025	27	91.4
Secondary school teachers...........	956	1,031	20	529	986	25	427	1,093	38	90.2
Special education teachers...........	337	951	15	271	944	17	65	977	54	96.6
Other teachers and instructors.......	336	905	39	187	729	63	149	1,055	55	69.1
Archivists, curators, and museum technicians.............................	33	–	–	20	–	–	13	–	–	–
Librarians..............................	149	919	31	121	905	36	28	–	–	–
Library technicians.....................	18	–	–	14	–	–	4	–	–	–
Teacher assistants.....................	571	479	11	501	475	13	70	501	25	94.8
Other education, training, and library workers...............................	131	1,031	35	91	992	34	39	–	–	–
Arts, design, entertainment, sports, and media occupations...............	1,510	988	17	649	884	22	861	1,118	30	79.1
Artists and related workers...........	63	1,032	88	25	–	–	38	–	–	–
Designers..............................	514	961	18	244	866	47	270	1,095	33	79.1
Actors.................................	18	–	–	10	–	–	8	–	–	–
Producers and directors..............	104	1,166	113	38	–	–	66	1,331	72	–

Table 2. Median usual weekly earnings of full-time wage and salary workers, by detailed occupation, 2013 annual averages — Continued
[Numbers in thousands]

Occupation	Total			Women			Men			Women's earnings as a percent-age of men's
	Number of workers	Median weekly earnings	Stan-dard error of median	Number of workers	Median weekly earnings	Stan-dard error of median	Number of workers	Median weekly earnings	Stan-dard error of median	
Athletes, coaches, umpires, and related workers..........................	115	889	55	29	–	–	86	934	73	–
Dancers and choreographers.........	1	–	–	1	–	–	0	–	–	–
Musicians, singers, and related workers.................................	46	–	–	13	–	–	33	–	–	–
Entertainers and performers, sports and related workers, all other......	9	–	–	7	–	–	2	–	–	–
Announcers.............................	18	–	–	6	–	–	13	–	–	–
News analysts, reporters and correspondents........................	68	1,041	114	22	–	–	46	–	–	–
Public relations specialists............	109	1,129	95	68	921	59	41	–	–	–
Editors..................................	112	1,092	144	59	988	40	53	1,239	87	79.7
Technical writers.......................	57	1,364	71	30	–	–	27	–	–	–
Writers and authors....................	79	996	57	40	–	–	39	–	–	–
Miscellaneous media and communication workers.............	32	–	–	24	–	–	8	–	–	–
Broadcast and sound engineering technicians and radio operators. ..	68	947	83	7	–	–	61	1,029	110	–
Photographers..........................	48	–	–	17	–	–	31	–	–	–
Television, video, and motion picture camera operators and editors......	45	–	–	6	–	–	38	–	–	–
Media and communication equipment workers, all other.......	1	–	–	0	–	–	1	–	–	–
Healthcare practitioners and technical occupations...........................	6,142	1,048	10	4,585	994	8	1,558	1,312	38	75.8
Chiropractors...........................	13	–	–	1	–	–	12	–	–	–
Dentists.................................	55	1,533	366	18	–	–	37	–	–	–
Dietitians and nutritionists.............	82	885	24	71	864	52	10	–	–	–
Optometrists............................	14	–	–	2	–	–	11	–	–	–
Pharmacists............................	215	1,960	110	117	1,802	168	98	2,092	22	86.1
Physicians and surgeons..............	667	1,885	24	241	1,497	109	426	2,087	228	71.7
Physician assistants...................	103	1,456	75	67	1,491	44	36	–	–	–
Podiatrists..............................	4	–	–	3	–	–	1	–	–	–
Audiologists............................	10	–	–	7	–	–	3	–	–	–
Occupational therapists...............	78	1,295	47	68	1,240	87	11	–	–	–
Physical therapists.....................	161	1,382	51	87	1,300	40	74	1,457	32	89.2
Radiation therapists....................	12	–	–	8	–	–	4	–	–	–
Recreational therapists................	10	–	–	8	–	–	2	–	–	–
Respiratory therapists.................	96	1,095	25	52	1,059	137	44	–	–	–
Speech-language pathologists........	98	1,218	77	93	1,191	93	5	–	–	–
Exercise physiologists.................	4	–	–	3	–	–	1	–	–	–
Therapists, all other...................	96	864	31	77	870	32	19	–	–	–
Veterinarians...........................	41	–	–	23	–	–	18	–	–	–
Registered nurses.....................	2,278	1,099	13	2,023	1,086	12	254	1,236	40	87.9
Nurse anesthetists.....................	22	–	–	14	–	–	7	–	–	–
Nurse midwives........................	3	–	–	3	–	–	0	–	–	–
Nurse practitioners....................	102	1,615	70	91	1,539	132	11	–	–	–
Health diagnosing and treating practitioners, all other..............	7	–	–	6	–	–	1	–	–	–
Clinical laboratory technologists and technicians...........................	307	891	32	226	858	86	81	980	112	87.6
Dental hygienists......................	82	1,005	51	80	1,011	48	2	–	–	–
Diagnostic related technologists and technicians...........................	287	919	21	195	909	23	92	959	71	94.8
Emergency medical technicians and paramedics..........................	140	796	56	58	785	42	82	832	108	94.4

Table 2. Median usual weekly earnings of full-time wage and salary workers, by detailed occupation, 2013 annual averages — Continued

[Numbers in thousands]

Occupation	Total			Women			Men			Women's earnings as a percent- age of men's
	Number of workers	Median weekly earnings	Stan- dard error of median	Number of workers	Median weekly earnings	Stan- dard error of median	Number of workers	Median weekly earnings	Stan- dard error of median	
Health practitioner support technologists and technicians......	416	619	15	337	613	14	78	664	54	92.3
Licensed practical and licensed vocational nurses...................	444	741	15	404	732	16	40	–	–	–
Medical records and health information technicians..............	78	612	54	72	595	58	6	–	–	–
Opticians, dispensing.................	37	–	–	25	–	–	13	–	–	–
Miscellaneous health technologists and technicians......................	114	849	65	73	782	37	41	–	–	–
Other healthcare practitioners and technical occupations..............	69	1,065	32	31	–	–	37	–	–	–
Service occupations..........................	15,052	493	2	7,456	452	3	7,597	555	7	81.4
Healthcare support occupations..........	2,324	491	5	2,020	486	5	304	546	23	89.0
Nursing, psychiatric, and home health aides..................................	1,393	457	6	1,207	450	7	186	499	23	90.2
Occupational therapy assistants and aides.................................	11	–	–	11	–	–	0	–	–	–
Physical therapist assistants and aides.................................	39	–	–	26	–	–	13	–	–	–
Massage therapists......................	48	–	–	32	–	–	15	–	–	–
Dental assistants.........................	181	571	17	174	571	17	7	–	–	–
Medical assistants.......................	365	531	17	339	523	12	26	–	–	–
Medical transcriptionists.................	34	–	–	33	–	–	1	–	–	–
Pharmacy aides..........................	22	–	–	19	–	–	3	–	–	–
Veterinary assistants and laboratory animal caretakers.....................	23	–	–	20	–	–	3	–	–	–
Phlebotomists.............................	97	583	24	77	573	20	19	–	–	–
Miscellaneous healthcare support occupations, including medical equipment preparers...............	112	462	20	81	440	18	31	–	–	–
Protective service occupations.............	2,685	783	13	512	643	24	2,172	824	16	78.0
First-line supervisors of correctional officers.................................	33	–	–	5	–	–	28	–	–	–
First-line supervisors of police and detectives..............................	114	1,139	42	17	–	–	97	1,182	200	–
First-line supervisors of fire fighting and prevention workers..............	60	1,082	337	0	–	–	60	1,082	337	–
First-line supervisors of protective service workers, all other.............	82	785	36	25	–	–	57	788	49	–
Firefighters.................................	294	996	47	9	–	–	285	1,000	48	–
Fire inspectors...........................	18	–	–	1	–	–	17	–	–	–
Bailiffs, correctional officers, and jailers..................................	418	683	21	120	599	18	298	729	28	82.2
Detectives and criminal investigators...	159	1,054	147	30	–	–	128	1,120	108	–
Fish and game wardens.................	2	–	–	1	–	–	1	–	–	–
Parking enforcement workers...........	5	–	–	2	–	–	4	–	–	–
Police and sheriff's patrol officers.......	682	1,007	41	89	881	39	593	1,032	50	85.4
Transit and railroad police..............	2	–	–	0	–	–	2	–	–	–
Animal control workers...................	10	–	–	4	–	–	6	–	–	–
Private detectives and investigators....	72	948	50	32	–	–	40	–	–	–
Security guards and gaming surveillance officers...................	643	532	18	125	500	16	517	549	22	91.1
Crossing guards..........................	14	–	–	7	–	–	7	–	–	–
Transportation security screeners......	25	–	–	10	–	–	16	–	–	–
Lifeguards and other recreational, and all other protective service workers...	52	484	35	36	–	–	16	–	–	–

Table 2. Median usual weekly earnings of full-time wage and salary workers, by detailed occupation, 2013 annual averages — Continued
[Numbers in thousands]

Occupation	Total			Women			Men			Women's earnings as a percent- age of men's
	Number of workers	Median weekly earnings	Stan- dard error of median	Number of workers	Median weekly earnings	Stan- dard error of median	Number of workers	Median weekly earnings	Stan- dard error of median	
Food preparation and serving related occupations.................................	4,140	416	3	1,953	400	4	2,187	437	9	91.5
Chefs and head cooks...................	351	574	20	69	510	19	282	589	22	86.6
First-line supervisors of food preparation and serving workers.....	423	491	17	249	448	18	174	580	27	77.2
Cooks.......................................	1,209	402	4	418	382	8	791	411	5	92.9
Food preparation workers...............	398	387	7	191	380	10	206	392	8	96.9
Bartenders.................................	207	513	19	109	483	20	98	594	21	81.3
Combined food preparation and serving workers, including fast food......................................	175	384	14	107	370	20	68	413	28	89.6
Counter attendants, cafeteria, food concession, and coffee shop........	57	320	15	43	–	–	14	–	–	–
Waiters and waitresses..................	883	413	6	558	400	8	325	449	30	89.1
Food servers, nonrestaurant...........	109	458	33	74	410	22	36	–	–	–
Dining room and cafeteria attendants and bartender helpers................	130	412	16	55	398	20	76	426	26	93.4
Dishwashers..............................	127	356	10	21	–	–	106	359	10	–
Hosts and hostesses, restaurant, lounge, and coffee shop..............	69	393	22	60	391	23	9	–	–	–
Food preparation and serving related workers, all other......................	1	–	–	0	–	–	1	–	–	–
Building and grounds cleaning and maintenance occupations...............	3,421	475	5	1,142	417	5	2,279	505	6	82.6
First-line supervisors of housekeeping and janitorial workers..................	186	638	43	78	511	20	108	801	23	63.8
First-line supervisors of landscaping, lawn service, and groundskeeping workers...................................	104	766	25	5	–	–	99	759	24	–
Janitors and building cleaners...........	1,537	487	7	421	418	8	1,116	517	8	80.9
Maids and housekeeping cleaners.....	733	413	6	605	406	7	128	467	31	86.9
Pest control workers......................	62	609	37	2	–	–	60	606	38	–
Grounds maintenance workers..........	799	445	15	31	–	–	768	441	15	–
Personal care and service occupations...	2,482	481	5	1,829	464	7	654	549	21	84.5
First-line supervisors of gaming workers...................................	97	755	21	48	–	–	49	–	–	–
First-line supervisors of personal service workers........................	72	595	22	44	–	–	28	–	–	–
Animal trainers............................	8	–	–	5	–	–	3	–	–	–
Nonfarm animal caretakers..............	78	458	25	57	468	30	22	–	–	–
Gaming services workers................	74	651	48	39	–	–	35	–	–	–
Motion picture projectionists............	3	–	–	2	–	–	1	–	–	–
Ushers, lobby attendants, and ticket takers.....................................	9	–	–	5	–	–	4	–	–	–
Miscellaneous entertainment attendants and related workers.......	74	419	48	37	–	–	37	–	–	–
Embalmers and funeral attendants.....	10	–	–	6	–	–	5	–	–	–
Morticians, undertakers, and funeral directors.................................	28	–	–	7	–	–	21	–	–	–
Barbers....................................	60	389	57	9	–	–	51	369	31	–
Hairdressers, hairstylists, and cosmetologists.........................	329	488	10	308	485	10	21	–	–	–
Miscellaneous personal appearance workers...................................	170	495	17	136	480	21	34	–	–	–
Baggage porters, bellhops, and concierges..............................	71	491	27	10	–	–	60	495	30	–
Tour and travel guides..................	21	–	–	13	–	–	8	–	–	–

Table 2. Median usual weekly earnings of full-time wage and salary workers, by detailed occupation, 2013 annual averages — Continued

[Numbers in thousands]

Occupation	Total			Women			Men			Women's earnings as a percent- age of men's
	Number of workers	Median weekly earnings	Stan- dard error of median	Number of workers	Median weekly earnings	Stan- dard error of median	Number of workers	Median weekly earnings	Stan- dard error of median	
Childcare workers........................	441	418	9	410	418	9	31	–	–	–
Personal care aides......................	657	449	11	539	445	11	119	470	26	94.7
Recreation and fitness workers.........	213	538	32	123	523	29	90	561	49	93.2
Residential advisors......................	32	–	–	18	–	–	13	–	–	–
Personal care and service workers, all other........................	36	–	–	13	–	–	22	–	–	–
Sales and office occupations................	23,120	659	3	14,008	615	2	9,112	756	5	81.3
Sales and related occupations............	9,376	708	7	4,005	566	9	5,371	835	11	67.8
First-line supervisors of retail sales workers..........................	2,320	709	11	981	612	9	1,338	778	15	78.7
First-line supervisors of non-retail sales workers.........................	757	980	31	217	934	49	540	1,004	41	93.0
Cashiers...............................	1,350	392	6	932	379	6	418	426	16	89.0
Counter and rental clerks...............	58	612	39	24	–	–	35	–	–	–
Parts salespersons......................	83	663	32	8	–	–	75	665	36	–
Retail salespersons......................	1,829	598	10	737	485	8	1,092	719	18	67.5
Advertising sales agents.................	207	938	50	96	868	47	110	1,005	71	86.4
Insurance sales agents..................	431	838	28	216	733	17	216	1,029	55	71.2
Securities, commodities, and financial services sales agents.................	219	1,119	70	75	863	104	145	1,389	177	62.1
Travel agents............................	42	–	–	32	–	–	10	–	–	–
Sales representatives, services, all other.................................	348	948	32	106	766	34	242	1,013	59	75.6
Sales representatives, wholesale and manufacturing..........................	1,085	1,042	42	247	859	34	838	1,131	21	76.0
Models, demonstrators, and product promoters............................	24	–	–	13	–	–	11	–	–	–
Real estate brokers and sales agents..	357	809	53	209	756	52	148	928	81	81.5
Sales engineers..........................	33	–	–	4	–	–	29	–	–	–
Telemarketers...........................	49	–	–	32	–	–	18	–	–	–
Door-to-door sales workers, news and street vendors, and related workers..............................	34	–	–	11	–	–	23	–	–	–
Sales and related workers, all other....	150	915	32	65	724	64	85	1,161	47	62.4
Office and administrative support occupations............................	13,744	638	3	10,003	628	3	3,741	673	9	93.3
First-line supervisors of office and administrative support workers.......	1,224	772	11	828	748	12	395	846	37	88.4
Switchboard operators, including answering service.....................	22	–	–	16	–	–	6	–	–	–
Telephone operators......................	20	–	–	17	–	–	3	–	–	–
Communications equipment operators, all other................................	2	–	–	2	–	–	0			
Bill and account collectors..............	156	599	18	111	586	15	45	–	–	–
Billing and posting clerks...............	422	637	14	380	629	13	42	–	–	–
Bookkeeping, accounting, and auditing clerks.................................	804	677	15	702	670	15	102	751	45	89.2
Gaming cage workers....................	12	–	–	6	–	–	6	–	–	–
Payroll and timekeeping clerks..........	128	731	22	118	727	23	9	–	–	–
Procurement clerks......................	30	–	–	18	–	–	12	–	–	–
Tellers..................................	265	494	11	229	494	11	36	–	–	–
Financial clerks, all other..............	54	686	58	34	–	–	20	–	–	–
Brokerage clerks.........................	2	–	–	1	–	–	1	–	–	–
Correspondence clerks..................	12	–	–	7	–	–	4	–	–	–
Court, municipal, and license clerks....	74	676	54	53	665	64	21	–	–	–

Table 2. Median usual weekly earnings of full-time wage and salary workers, by detailed occupation, 2013 annual averages — Continued

[Numbers in thousands]

Occupation	Total			Women			Men			Women's earnings as a percent-age of men's
	Number of workers	Median weekly earnings	Standard error of median	Number of workers	Median weekly earnings	Standard error of median	Number of workers	Median weekly earnings	Standard error of median	
Credit authorizers, checkers, and clerks..................	40	–	–	30	–	–	10	–	–	–
Customer service representatives......	1,615	621	8	1,068	616	7	547	639	19	96.4
Eligibility interviewers, government programs..............................	75	778	58	60	746	54	15	–	–	–
File clerks................................	182	625	20	140	604	21	42	–	–	–
Hotel, motel, and resort desk clerks....	71	418	14	50	417	16	21	–	–	–
Interviewers, except eligibility and loan..	110	621	32	89	605	31	21	–	–	–
Library assistants, clerical...............	50	559	31	42	–	–	8	–	–	–
Loan interviewers and clerks............	158	719	29	129	688	31	29	–	–	–
New accounts clerks.....................	29	–	–	26	–	–	3	–	–	–
Order clerks..............................	79	583	36	42	–	–	37	–	–	–
Human resources assistants, except payroll and timekeeping..............	129	877	40	103	873	46	26	–	–	–
Receptionists and information clerks...	901	536	9	828	527	9	73	600	24	87.8
Reservation and transportation ticket agents and travel clerks..............	100	699	41	54	620	18	46	–	–	–
Information and record clerks, all other..	85	710	33	62	727	25	23	–	–	–
Cargo and freight agents................	26	–	–	9	–	–	17	–	–	–
Couriers and messengers..............	127	624	38	16	–	–	112	616	25	–
Dispatchers..............................	246	676	27	140	617	33	107	747	31	82.6
Meter readers, utilities...................	24	–	–	6	–	–	19	–	–	–
Postal service clerks.....................	90	968	27	45	–	–	45	–	–	–
Postal service mail carriers.............	277	964	19	101	878	59	176	1,012	22	86.8
Postal service mail sorters, processors, and processing machine operators...............................	70	873	62	35	–	–	35	–	–	–
Production, planning, and expediting clerks....................................	272	745	30	148	690	28	124	864	75	79.9
Shipping, receiving, and traffic clerks...	493	539	20	151	524	21	342	547	26	95.8
Stock clerks and order fillers............	918	496	10	321	484	15	596	503	13	96.2
Weighers, measurers, checkers, and samplers, recordkeeping..............	74	624	32	37	–	–	37	–	–	–
Secretaries and administrative assistants................................	2,232	681	8	2,113	677	7	120	772	40	87.7
Computer operators......................	80	732	61	39	–	–	41	–	–	–
Data entry keyers........................	235	634	19	189	632	20	46	–	–	–
Word processors and typists............	90	621	25	82	607	23	8	–	–	–
Desktop publishers.......................	0	–	–	0	–	–	0	–	–	–
Insurance claims and policy processing clerks......................	252	652	26	206	631	27	46	–	–	–
Mail clerks and mail machine operators, except postal service......	48	–	–	22	–	–	26	–	–	–
Office clerks, general....................	852	598	8	734	596	8	118	620	71	96.1
Office machine operators, except computer.................................	35	–	–	21	–	–	14	–	–	–
Proofreaders and copy markers........	3	–	–	3	–	–	0	–	–	–
Statistical assistants.....................	18	–	–	10	–	–	8	–	–	–
Office and administrative support workers, all other......................	431	724	22	331	695	30	100	795	70	87.4
Natural resources, construction, and maintenance occupations..................	10,341	747	6	434	578	19	9,906	757	6	76.4
Farming, fishing, and forestry occupations.............................	720	448	12	144	368	8	576	472	12	78.0

Table 2. Median usual weekly earnings of full-time wage and salary workers, by detailed occupation, 2013 annual averages — Continued

[Numbers in thousands]

Occupation	Total			Women			Men			Women's earnings as a percent-age of men's
	Number of workers	Median weekly earnings	Stan-dard error of median	Number of workers	Median weekly earnings	Stan-dard error of median	Number of workers	Median weekly earnings	Stan-dard error of median	
First-line supervisors of farming, fishing, and forestry workers..........	34	–	–	8	–	–	25	–	–	–
Agricultural inspectors....................	11	–	–	3	–	–	8	–	–	–
Animal breeders............................	1	–	–	0	–	–	1	–	–	–
Graders and sorters, agricultural products.................................	91	416	20	57	389	22	34	–	–	–
Miscellaneous agricultural workers.....	516	428	13	71	352	10	445	447	15	78.7
Fishers and related fishing workers....	16	–	–	2	–	–	15	–	–	–
Hunters and trappers.....................	0	–	–	0	–	–	0	–	–	–
Forest and conservation workers.......	11	–	–	1	–	–	10	–	–	–
Logging workers...........................	39	–	–	1	–	–	37	–	–	–
Construction and extraction occupations.............................	5,353	732	9	112	654	31	5,242	736	10	88.9
First-line supervisors of construction trades and extraction workers........	509	990	28	8	–	–	501	996	27	–
Boilermakers..............................	14	–	–	0	–	–	14	–	–	–
Brickmasons, blockmasons, and stonemasons...........................	106	768	68	0	–	–	106	766	71	–
Carpenters.................................	712	657	21	10	–	–	703	659	23	–
Carpet, floor, and tile installers and finishers.................................	80	582	25	2	–	–	78	579	25	–
Cement masons, concrete finishers, and terrazzo workers..................	46	–	–	0	–	–	46	–	–	–
Construction laborers....................	1,087	594	9	29	–	–	1,058	592	9	–
Paving, surfacing, and tamping equipment operators..................	18	–	–	1	–	–	18	–	–	–
Pile-driver operators......................	1	–	–	0	–	–	1	–	–	–
Operating engineers and other construction equipment operators....	322	801	35	4	–	–	317	804	34	–
Drywall installers, ceiling tile installers, and tapers.............................	81	521	19	0	–	–	81	522	20	–
Electricians.................................	641	949	23	11	–	–	630	952	23	–
Glaziers.....................................	31	–	–	0	–	–	31	–	–	–
Insulation workers.........................	44	–	–	2	–	–	42	–	–	–
Painters, construction and maintenance...........................	331	576	19	14	–	–	318	579	18	–
Paperhangers..............................	0	–	–	0	–	–	0	–	–	–
Pipelayers, plumbers, pipefitters, and steamfitters.............................	450	909	17	4	–	–	447	912	17	–
Plasterers and stucco masons..........	24	–	–	0	–	–	24	–	–	–
Reinforcing iron and rebar workers.....	8	–	–	0	–	–	8	–	–	–
Roofers.....................................	133	566	32	0	–	–	133	566	32	–
Sheet metal workers.....................	100	789	33	7	–	–	93	797	37	–
Structural iron and steel workers.......	38	–	–	0	–	–	38	–	–	–
Solar photovoltaic installers.............	6	–	–	0	–	–	5	–	–	–
Helpers, construction trades.............	46	–	–	2	–	–	44	–	–	–
Construction and building inspectors...	73	903	69	5	–	–	67	920	73	–
Elevator installers and repairers........	25	–	–	0	–	–	25	–	–	–
Fence erectors.............................	24	–	–	0	–	–	24	–	–	–
Hazardous materials removal workers...............................	28	–	–	8	–	–	20	–	–	–
Highway maintenance workers..........	95	709	24	0	–	–	95	709	24	–
Rail-track laying and maintenance equipment operators..................	16	–	–	0	–	–	16	–	–	–
Septic tank servicers and sewer pipe cleaners.................................	7	–	–	0	–	–	7	–	–	–

Table 2. Median usual weekly earnings of full-time wage and salary workers, by detailed occupation, 2013 annual averages — Continued
[Numbers in thousands]

Occupation	Total			Women			Men			Women's earnings as a percent- age of men's
	Number of workers	Median weekly earnings	Stan- dard error of median	Number of workers	Median weekly earnings	Stan- dard error of median	Number of workers	Median weekly earnings	Stan- dard error of median	
Miscellaneous construction and related workers..................................	21	–	–	0	–	–	21	–	–	–
Derrick, rotary drill, and service unit operators, oil, gas, and mining.......	38	–	–	0	–	–	38	–	–	–
Earth drillers, except oil and gas........	26	–	–	0	–	–	26	–	–	–
Explosives workers, ordnance handling experts, and blasters........	8	–	–	0	–	–	8	–	–	–
Mining machine operators..............	60	1,014	263	2	–	–	58	1,084	305	–
Roof bolters, mining.....................	2	–	–	0	–	–	2	–	–	–
Roustabouts, oil and gas................	12	–	–	0	–	–	12	–	–	–
Helpers--extraction workers.............	3	–	–	0	–	–	3	–	–	–
Other extraction workers................	86	920	96	3	–	–	83	909	75	–
Installation, maintenance, and repair occupations..............................	4,268	821	8	179	710	27	4,089	824	9	86.2
First-line supervisors of mechanics, installers, and repairers...............	258	980	52	29	–	–	229	990	58	–
Computer, automated teller, and office machine repairers.....................	240	875	35	29	–	–	211	894	31	–
Radio and telecommunications equipment installers and repairers. ..	122	1,025	52	13	–	–	108	1,021	52	–
Avionics technicians......................	10	–	–	4	–	–	6	–	–	–
Electric motor, power tool, and related repairers.................................	24	–	–	1	–	–	23	–	–	–
Electrical and electronics installers and repairers, transportation equipment..	6	–	–	0	–	–	6	–	–	–
Electrical and electronics repairers, industrial and utility....................	13	–	–	1	–	–	12	–	–	–
Electronic equipment installers and repairers, motor vehicles..............	24	–	–	2	–	–	22	–	–	–
Electronic home entertainment equipment installers and repairers. ..	42	–	–	1	–	–	41	–	–	–
Security and fire alarm systems installers................................	60	780	20	2	–	–	58	780	19	–
Aircraft mechanics and service technicians.............................	155	978	45	3	–	–	152	974	45	–
Automotive body and related repairers................................	124	687	17	1	–	–	123	688	16	–
Automotive glass installers and repairers................................	20	–	–	0	–	–	20	–	–	–
Automotive service technicians and mechanics.............................	672	713	15	13	–	–	659	714	15	–
Bus and truck mechanics and diesel engine specialists.....................	302	794	24	0	–	–	301	795	24	–
Heavy vehicle and mobile equipment service technicians and mechanics...	196	867	36	1	–	–	195	868	36	–
Small engine mechanics................	32	–	–	1	–	–	31	–	–	–
Miscellaneous vehicle and mobile equipment mechanics, installers, and repairers............................	74	468	100	2	–	–	72	480	37	–
Control and valve installers and repairers................................	24	–	–	2	–	–	22	–	–	–
Heating, air conditioning, and refrigeration mechanics and installers...............................	316	792	38	3	–	–	313	791	40	–
Home appliance repairers..............	38	–	–	0	–	–	38	–	–	–
Industrial and refractory machinery mechanics.............................	434	896	18	20	–	–	414	899	18	–

Table 2. Median usual weekly earnings of full-time wage and salary workers, by detailed occupation, 2013 annual averages — Continued

[Numbers in thousands]

Occupation	Total			Women			Men			Women's earnings as a percent-age of men's
	Number of workers	Median weekly earnings	Standard error of median	Number of workers	Median weekly earnings	Standard error of median	Number of workers	Median weekly earnings	Standard error of median	
Maintenance and repair workers, general................................	405	805	17	18	–	–	386	807	17	–
Maintenance workers, machinery.......	33	–	–	3	–	–	30	–	–	–
Millwrights................................	62	1,019	63	1	–	–	61	1,025	118	–
Electrical power-line installers and repairers................................	113	922	62	1	–	–	112	929	72	–
Telecommunications line installers and repairers................................	177	930	32	6	–	–	172	929	34	–
Precision instrument and equipment repairers................................	58	951	24	7	–	–	51	956	23	–
Wind turbine service technicians........	3	–	–	2	–	–	1	–	–	–
Coin, vending, and amusement machine servicers and repairers.....	32	–	–	4	–	–	28	–	–	–
Commercial divers........................	2	–	–	0	–	–	1	–	–	–
Locksmiths and safe repairers..........	17	–	–	0	–	–	16	–	–	–
Manufactured building and mobile home installers........................	10	–	–	0	–	–	10	–	–	–
Riggers...................................	13	–	–	0	–	–	13	–	–	–
Signal and track switch repairers.......	5	–	–	0	–	–	5	–	–	–
Helpers--installation, maintenance, and repair workers...........................	18	–	–	3	–	–	15	–	–	–
Other installation, maintenance, and repair workers...........................	135	667	27	6	–	–	129	674	44	–
Production, transportation, and material moving occupations.........................	13,930	621	3	2,840	498	4	11,090	674	5	73.9
Production occupations....................	7,307	623	5	1,925	498	5	5,382	697	6	71.4
First-line supervisors of production and operating workers.....................	675	902	25	125	682	54	550	952	20	71.6
Aircraft structure, surfaces, rigging, and systems assemblers..............	16	–	–	3	–	–	13	–	–	–
Electrical, electronics, and electromechanical assemblers........	126	503	17	61	490	19	64	522	68	93.9
Engine and other machine assemblers.............................	19	–	–	2	–	–	17	–	–	–
Structural metal fabricators and fitters...................................	21	–	–	0	–	–	21	–	–	–
Miscellaneous assemblers and fabricators..............................	900	564	14	335	493	9	566	610	10	80.8
Bakers....................................	117	505	20	61	524	29	56	488	27	107.4
Butchers and other meat, poultry, and fish processing workers..............	284	506	10	73	476	15	211	525	20	90.7
Food and tobacco roasting, baking, and drying machine operators and tenders.................................	6	–	–	2	–	–	4	–	–	–
Food batchmakers.......................	66	516	47	33	–	–	33	–	–	–
Food cooking machine operators and tenders.................................	6	–	–	3	–	–	3	–	–	–
Food processing workers, all other.....	113	571	29	35	–	–	78	635	56	–
Computer control programmers and operators...............................	69	849	37	2	–	–	66	859	37	–
Extruding and drawing machine setters, operators, and tenders, metal and plastic......................	16	–	–	2	–	–	14	–	–	–
Forging machine setters, operators, and tenders, metal and plastic.......	9	–	–	0	–	–	9	–	–	–
Rolling machine setters, operators, and tenders, metal and plastic.......	3	–	–	0	–	–	3	–	–	–

Table 2. Median usual weekly earnings of full-time wage and salary workers, by detailed occupation, 2013 annual averages — Continued
[Numbers in thousands]

Occupation	Total			Women			Men			Women's earnings as a percent-age of men's
	Number of workers	Median weekly earnings	Stan-dard error of median	Number of workers	Median weekly earnings	Stan-dard error of median	Number of workers	Median weekly earnings	Stan-dard error of median	
Cutting, punching, and press machine setters, operators, and tenders, metal and plastic......................	70	545	38	10	–	–	60	532	41	–
Drilling and boring machine tool setters, operators, and tenders, metal and plastic......................	1	–	–	0	–	–	1	–	–	–
Grinding, lapping, polishing, and buffing machine tool setters, operators, and tenders, metal and plastic....................	50	610	37	6	–	–	44	–	–	–
Lathe and turning machine tool setters, operators, and tenders, metal and plastic......................	11	–	–	3	–	–	8	–	–	–
Milling and planing machine setters, operators, and tenders, metal and plastic...................................	5	–	–	0	–	–	5	–	–	–
Machinists................................	388	777	22	21	–	–	367	795	25	–
Metal furnace operators, tenders, pourers, and casters.................	23	–	–	0	–	–	23	–	–	–
Model makers and patternmakers, metal and plastic......................	3	–	–	1	–	–	2	–	–	–
Molders and molding machine setters, operators, and tenders, metal and plastic....................	51	717	65	13	–	–	38	–	–	–
Multiple machine tool setters, operators, and tenders, metal and plastic....................	4	–	–	1	–	–	3	–	–	–
Tool and die makers......................	55	908	50	1	–	–	55	911	50	–
Welding, soldering, and brazing workers................................	524	723	17	25	–	–	499	730	15	–
Heat treating equipment setters, operators, and tenders, metal and plastic...................................	9	–	–	1	–	–	8	–	–	–
Layout workers, metal and plastic......	4	–	–	0	–	–	3	–	–	–
Plating and coating machine setters, operators, and tenders, metal and plastic...................................	16	–	–	1	–	–	15	–	–	–
Tool grinders, filers, and sharpeners...	4	–	–	0	–	–	4	–	–	–
Metal workers and plastic workers, all other...................................	323	592	19	66	557	24	257	606	24	91.9
Prepress technicians and workers......	25	–	–	9	–	–	17	–	–	–
Printing press operators..................	175	656	55	30	–	–	145	703	30	–
Print binding and finishing workers.....	22	–	–	13	–	–	8	–	–	–
Laundry and dry-cleaning workers......	121	385	15	71	360	14	50	425	32	84.7
Pressers, textile, garment, and related materials................................	35	–	–	17	–	–	18	–	–	–
Sewing machine operators..............	121	405	18	91	405	23	29	–	–	–
Shoe and leather workers and repairers................................	5	–	–	1	–	–	4	–	–	–
Shoe machine operators and tenders..	3	–	–	1	–	–	1	–	–	–
Tailors, dressmakers, and sewers......	42	–	–	28	–	–	13	–	–	–
Textile bleaching and dyeing machine operators and tenders.................	2	–	–	1	–	–	1	–	–	–
Textile cutting machine setters, operators, and tenders...............	5	–	–	1	–	–	5	–	–	–
Textile knitting and weaving machine setters, operators, and tenders.......	3	–	–	3	–	–	0	–	–	–

Table 2. Median usual weekly earnings of full-time wage and salary workers, by detailed occupation, 2013 annual averages — Continued
[Numbers in thousands]

Occupation	Total			Women			Men			Women's earnings as a percent-age of men's
	Number of workers	Median weekly earnings	Stan-dard error of median	Number of workers	Median weekly earnings	Stan-dard error of median	Number of workers	Median weekly earnings	Stan-dard error of median	
Textile winding, twisting, and drawing out machine setters, operators, and tenders..................................	12	–	–	5	–	–	7	–	–	–
Extruding and forming machine setters, operators, and tenders, synthetic and glass fibers.............	1	–	–	0	–	–	1	–	–	–
Fabric and apparel patternmakers......	1	–	–	1	–	–	0	–	–	–
Upholsterers..................................	19	–	–	2	–	–	17	–	–	–
Textile, apparel, and furnishings workers, all other......................	12	–	–	3	–	–	8	–	–	–
Cabinetmakers and bench carpenters.................................	28	–	–	0	–	–	27	–	–	–
Furniture finishers.........................	5	–	–	1	–	–	4	–	–	–
Model makers and patternmakers, wood..................................	0	–	–	0	–	–	0	–	–	–
Sawing machine setters, operators, and tenders, wood....................	25	–	–	2	–	–	23	–	–	–
Woodworking machine setters, operators, and tenders, except sawing..................................	18	–	–	4	–	–	14	–	–	–
Woodworkers, all other..................	9	–	–	1	–	–	8	–	–	–
Power plant operators, distributors, and dispatchers.........................	41	–	–	6	–	–	35	–	–	–
Stationary engineers and boiler operators.................................	90	903	37	5	–	–	84	922	44	–
Water and wastewater treatment plant and system operators.................	68	828	42	4	–	–	64	829	42	–
Miscellaneous plant and system operators.................................	41	–	–	2	–	–	40	–	–	–
Chemical processing machine setters, operators, and tenders...............	46	–	–	5	–	–	41	–	–	–
Crushing, grinding, polishing, mixing, and blending workers..................	88	716	48	11	–	–	77	807	100	–
Cutting workers............................	40	–	–	10	–	–	30	–	–	–
Extruding, forming, pressing, and compacting machine setters, operators, and tenders...............	31	–	–	5	–	–	26	–	–	–
Furnace, kiln, oven, drier, and kettle operators and tenders.................	10	–	–	0	–	–	10	–	–	–
Inspectors, testers, sorters, samplers, and weighers...........................	650	741	15	211	583	27	439	835	32	69.8
Jewelers and precious stone and metal workers...........................	23	–	–	6	–	–	17	–	–	–
Medical, dental, and ophthalmic laboratory technicians..................	67	701	27	33	–	–	34	–	–	–
Packaging and filling machine operators and tenders.................	297	488	9	159	429	20	137	537	26	79.9
Painting workers...........................	125	664	36	17	–	–	108	673	32	–
Photographic process workers and processing machine operators........	26	–	–	11	–	–	15	–	–	–
Semiconductor processors..............	2	–	–	1	–	–	1	–	–	–
Adhesive bonding machine operators and tenders.............................	11	–	–	5	–	–	5	–	–	–
Cleaning, washing, and metal pickling equipment operators and tenders....	3	–	–	1	–	–	2	–	–	–
Cooling and freezing equipment operators and tenders.................	1	–	–	0	–	–	1	–	–	–
Etchers and engravers..................	2	–	–	0	–	–	2	–	–	–

Table 2. Median usual weekly earnings of full-time wage and salary workers, by detailed occupation, 2013 annual averages — Continued

[Numbers in thousands]

Occupation	Total			Women			Men			Women's earnings as a percent-age of men's
	Number of workers	Median weekly earnings	Stan-dard error of median	Number of workers	Median weekly earnings	Stan-dard error of median	Number of workers	Median weekly earnings	Stan-dard error of median	
Molders, shapers, and casters, except metal and plastic......................	31	–	–	3	–	–	28	–	–	–
Paper goods machine setters, operators, and tenders...............	21	–	–	3	–	–	18	–	–	–
Tire builders..............................	23	–	–	7	–	–	16	–	–	–
Helpers--production workers............	29	–	–	9	–	–	20	–	–	–
Production workers, all other............	866	586	10	236	501	12	630	619	11	80.9
Transportation and material moving occupations................................	6,623	619	5	916	497	8	5,707	645	8	77.1
Supervisors of transportation and material moving workers..............	165	882	47	38	–	–	126	930	24	–
Aircraft pilots and flight engineers......	100	1,845	40	7	–	–	93	1,859	59	–
Air traffic controllers and airfield operations specialists..................	41	–	–	5	–	–	37	–	–	–
Flight attendants........................	69	767	31	54	749	26	16	–	–	–
Ambulance drivers and attendants, except emergency medical technicians............................	12	–	–	3	–	–	9	–	–	–
Bus drivers..............................	339	579	17	147	556	35	192	597	28	93.1
Driver/sales workers and truck drivers..................................	2,587	730	10	106	583	34	2,482	738	10	79.0
Taxi drivers and chauffeurs..............	202	521	19	30	–	–	172	540	96	–
Motor vehicle operators, all other.......	39	–	–	3	–	–	37	–	–	–
Locomotive engineers and operators...	50	1,396	72	2	–	–	48	–	–	–
Railroad brake, signal, and switch operators............................	12	–	–	0	–	–	11	–	–	–
Railroad conductors and yardmasters..	46	–	–	3	–	–	43	–	–	–
Subway, streetcar, and other rail transportation workers................	5	–	–	0	–	–	5	–	–	–
Sailors and marine oilers...............	29	–	–	1	–	–	28	–	–	–
Ship and boat captains and operators............................	32	–	–	0	–	–	32	–	–	–
Ship engineers.........................	7	–	–	0	–	–	7	–	–	–
Bridge and lock tenders..................	5	–	–	0	–	–	5	–	–	–
Parking lot attendants...................	50	423	18	7	–	–	43	–	–	–
Automotive and watercraft service attendants............................	78	398	12	12	–	–	67	403	14	–
Transportation inspectors...............	41	–	–	6	–	–	35	–	–	–
Transportation attendants, except flight attendants............................	30	–	–	16	–	–	14	–	–	–
Other transportation workers............	17	–	–	1	–	–	15	–	–	–
Conveyor operators and tenders........	4	–	–	1	–	–	3	–	–	–
Crane and tower operators..............	70	846	191	1	–	–	69	871	214	–
Dredge, excavating, and loading machine operators....................	28	–	–	0	–	–	28	–	–	–
Hoist and winch operators..............	7	–	–	0	–	–	7	–	–	–
Industrial truck and tractor operators...	542	559	17	32	–	–	510	559	18	–
Cleaners of vehicles and equipment. ..	235	429	15	28	–	–	206	434	15	–
Laborers and freight, stock, and material movers, hand..............	1,277	511	6	221	421	13	1,056	524	11	80.3
Machine feeders and offbearers........	20	–	–	4	–	–	15	–	–	–
Packers and packagers, hand..........	331	422	11	182	416	14	149	434	28	95.9
Pumping station operators..............	24	–	–	0	–	–	24	–	–	–
Refuse and recyclable material collectors................................	75	550	37	1	–	–	74	555	37	–

Table 2. Median usual weekly earnings of full-time wage and salary workers, by detailed occupation, 2013 annual averages — Continued

[Numbers in thousands]

Occupation	Total			Women			Men			Women's earnings as a percent-age of men's
	Number of workers	Median weekly earnings	Stan-dard error of median	Number of workers	Median weekly earnings	Stan-dard error of median	Number of workers	Median weekly earnings	Stan-dard error of median	
Mine shuttle car operators...............	3	–	–	0	–	–	3	–	–	–
Tank car, truck, and ship loaders.......	6	–	–	0	–	–	6	–	–	–
Material moving workers, all other......	45	–	–	5	–	–	41	–	–	–

Note: Median earnings are not shown where employment is less than 50,000. Women's earnings as a percentage of men's are not shown where employment for either women or men is less than 50,000. Dash indicates no data or data that do not meet publication criteria.
Source: U.S. Bureau of Labor Statistics.

Table 3. Median usual weekly earnings of full-time wage and salary workers, by state, 2013 annual averages

State	Total			Women			Men			Women's earnings as a percentage of men's
	Number of workers (in thousands)	Median weekly earnings	Standard error of median	Number of workers (in thousands)	Median weekly earnings	Standard error of median	Number of workers (in thousands)	Median weekly earnings	Standard error of median	
United States..................................	104,262	$776	$2	46,268	$706	$3	57,994	$860	$3	82.1
Alabama...	1,557	733	13	715	633	24	843	820	26	77.2
Alaska...	255	888	17	112	760	15	143	1,027	35	74.0
Arizona..	1,970	764	13	869	702	18	1,101	848	26	82.8
Arkansas..	912	660	14	400	607	15	512	705	19	86.1
California..	11,767	821	9	5,007	772	10	6,760	864	12	89.4
Colorado...	1,775	875	18	765	762	15	1,009	978	29	77.9
Connecticut.....................................	1,204	995	19	539	894	28	665	1,106	44	80.8
Delaware..	308	790	19	142	728	20	166	884	47	82.4
District of Columbia............................	271	1,152	22	138	1,100	55	133	1,212	61	90.8
Florida...	6,347	740	6	3,032	679	10	3,315	816	14	83.2
Georgia..	3,373	742	11	1,533	677	17	1,840	830	23	81.6
Hawaii...	449	783	18	204	727	18	245	863	28	84.2
Idaho..	469	707	14	180	649	19	290	741	14	87.6
Illinois...	4,293	816	13	1,945	727	13	2,348	891	15	81.6
Indiana..	2,149	733	12	936	650	15	1,212	830	28	78.3
Iowa...	1,124	757	13	509	671	18	615	861	22	77.9
Kansas..	983	743	13	430	653	22	554	826	26	79.1
Kentucky..	1,372	682	15	618	610	14	754	749	15	81.4
Louisiana..	1,422	692	12	627	591	13	794	808	32	73.1
Maine..	428	751	14	202	684	26	226	802	26	85.3
Maryland..	2,244	942	20	1,067	870	28	1,177	1,012	28	86.0
Massachusetts..................................	2,261	1,001	19	1,002	900	20	1,258	1,109	28	81.2
Michigan...	2,996	811	14	1,290	720	15	1,706	883	17	81.5
Minnesota.......................................	1,945	878	17	850	790	20	1,096	956	27	82.6
Mississippi......................................	868	660	18	411	593	17	457	739	23	80.2
Missouri...	2,075	743	14	948	665	17	1,127	852	31	78.1
Montana...	313	687	10	141	594	16	173	778	22	76.3
Nebraska..	697	738	13	311	668	17	386	801	17	83.4
Nevada..	951	702	11	421	649	14	529	745	16	87.1
New Hampshire.................................	489	884	19	215	788	32	274	956	23	82.4
New Jersey......................................	3,108	905	18	1,400	789	16	1,708	993	20	79.5
New Mexico.....................................	573	746	20	243	646	15	330	827	22	78.1
New York..	6,715	839	11	3,061	758	8	3,654	910	12	83.3
North Carolina..................................	3,164	705	12	1,428	635	12	1,735	768	15	82.7
North Dakota....................................	273	791	14	118	692	12	155	903	22	76.6
Ohio...	3,698	744	9	1,662	680	11	2,036	822	15	82.7
Oklahoma.......................................	1,295	677	12	565	591	12	730	756	18	78.2
Oregon..	1,143	781	21	494	705	15	649	873	27	80.8
Pennsylvania....................................	4,425	782	10	1,957	701	12	2,468	879	14	79.7
Rhode Island....................................	356	856	24	165	756	19	191	954	28	79.2
South Carolina..................................	1,545	703	15	719	622	14	826	785	13	79.2
South Dakota...................................	289	679	12	132	602	13	157	754	17	79.8
Tennessee......................................	2,033	687	20	886	629	16	1,147	745	17	84.4
Texas..	9,184	721	7	3,904	629	9	5,280	800	14	78.6
Utah...	970	754	11	366	642	16	604	864	22	74.3
Vermont...	216	777	15	99	745	19	117	816	26	91.3
Virginia..	2,988	897	18	1,357	808	21	1,631	971	26	83.2
Washington......................................	2,278	882	18	945	764	24	1,333	963	31	79.3
West Virginia....................................	572	740	15	253	633	25	319	847	25	74.7
Wisconsin.......................................	1,959	784	15	871	697	20	1,088	851	19	81.9
Wyoming..	211	847	20	83	671	22	128	978	20	68.6

Note: In general, the sampling error for the state estimates is considerably larger than it is for the national estimates; thus, comparisons of state estimates should be made with caution. Data shown are based on workers' state of residence; workers' reported earnings, however, may or may not be from a job located in the same state.
Source: U.S. Bureau of Labor Statistics.

Table 4. Median usual weekly earnings of part-time wage and salary workers, by selected demographic characteristics, 2013 annual averages

Characteristic	Total			Women			Men			Women's earnings as a percent-age of men's
	Number of workers (in thousands)	Median weekly earnings	Standard error of median	Number of workers (in thousands)	Median weekly earnings	Standard error of median	Number of workers (in thousands)	Median weekly earnings	Standard error of median	
Age										
Total, 16 years and older.....................	24,664	$237	$1	15,960	$241	$1	8,704	$230	$2	104.8
16 to 24 years..............................	8,375	181	2	4,673	177	2	3,702	186	2	95.2
16 to 19 years.........................	3,263	143	2	1,790	139	2	1,473	148	3	93.9
20 to 24 years.........................	5,112	207	2	2,883	205	2	2,229	209	3	98.1
25 years and older.........................	16,289	274	2	11,287	274	2	5,002	274	3	100.0
25 to 34 years.........................	4,281	264	3	2,740	265	4	1,541	264	4	100.4
35 to 44 years.........................	3,287	291	4	2,462	288	5	825	298	8	96.6
45 to 54 years.........................	3,358	289	4	2,623	285	5	735	309	11	92.2
55 to 64 years.........................	3,110	286	4	2,194	287	5	916	283	8	101.4
65 years and older.........................	2,253	243	4	1,268	236	6	985	252	7	93.7
Race and Hispanic or Latino Ethnicity										
White...	19,848	238	1	12,966	242	2	6,883	231	2	104.8
Black or African American...................	2,817	231	3	1,715	235	4	1,103	225	4	104.4
Asian...	1,188	246	6	779	251	8	409	236	11	106.4
Hispanic or Latino ethnicity..................	3,855	229	3	2,281	222	3	1,574	238	4	93.3
Marital Status										
Never married.................................	11,774	201	1	6,458	198	2	5,316	205	2	96.6
Married, spouse present.....................	9,532	288	3	6,991	287	3	2,541	291	5	98.6
Other marital status..........................	3,357	263	3	2,511	260	3	846	275	7	94.5
Divorced....................................	1,887	270	4	1,376	265	4	511	287	12	92.3
Separated..................................	826	260	6	595	258	7	231	266	11	97.0
Widowed....................................	645	246	8	540	245	8	104	249	24	98.4

Note: Estimates for the race groups shown (White, Black or African American, and Asian) do not sum to totals because data are not presented for all race groups. People of Hispanic or Latino ethnicity may be of any race; estimates for the race groups include Hispanics.
Source: U.S. Bureau of Labor Statistics.

Table 5. Median usual weekly earnings of wage and salary workers, by hours usually worked, 2013 annual averages

Hours of work	Total			Women			Men			Women's earnings as a percent-age of men's
	Number of workers (in thou-sands)	Median weekly earnings	Stan-dard error of median	Number of workers (in thou-sands)	Median weekly earnings	Stan-dard error of median	Number of workers (in thou-sands)	Median weekly earnings	Stan-dard error of median	
Total, 16 years and older......................	129,110	$665	$2	62,316	$584	$2	66,794	$764	$3	76.4
0 to 34 hours...............................	22,185	240	1	14,460	245	1	7,725	232	2	105.6
0 to 4 hours...............................	520	58	3	338	56	3	182	61	5	91.8
5 to 9 hours...............................	1,155	75	3	771	76	3	383	74	3	102.7
10 to 14 hours............................	1,785	113	1	1,168	115	2	617	109	2	105.5
15 to 19 hours............................	2,604	159	1	1,760	163	2	844	151	2	107.9
20 to 24 hours............................	6,654	217	1	4,307	223	2	2,347	209	2	106.7
25 to 29 hours............................	3,200	264	2	2,081	270	2	1,120	255	3	105.9
30 to 34 hours............................	6,268	336	3	4,035	352	4	2,232	315	3	111.7
35 hours and over........................	98,836	781	2	44,208	713	3	54,627	864	3	82.5
35 to 39 hours............................	8,128	495	4	5,380	507	5	2,748	466	7	108.8
40 hours...................................	70,466	732	2	32,504	691	3	37,963	771	3	89.6
41 hours and over........................	20,241	1,202	9	6,324	1,099	14	13,917	1,255	7	87.6
41 to 44 hours.........................	1,031	880	19	390	841	27	642	912	30	92.2
45 to 48 hours.........................	5,493	1,054	10	1,957	996	17	3,536	1,097	20	90.8
49 to 59 hours.........................	9,119	1,270	10	2,805	1,193	22	6,314	1,317	16	90.6
60 hours and over.....................	4,599	1,373	16	1,173	1,202	46	3,426	1,436	22	83.7
Hours vary...................................	8,089	463	9	3,648	324	6	4,441	618	12	52.4
Usually less than 35 hours.............	2,478	205	4	1,500	202	4	978	210	6	96.2
Usually 35 or more hours...............	5,427	672	13	2,060	496	12	3,367	791	17	62.7

Note: Data refer to the sole or principal job of full-time and part-time workers. Estimates for the "hours vary" groups do not sum to totals because data are not presented for a small number of multiple jobholders whose usual number of hours on the principal job is not identifiable.
Source: U.S. Bureau of Labor Statistics.

Table 6. Distribution of full-time wage and salary workers, by usual weekly earnings and selected demographic characteristics, 2013 annual averages
[In thousands]

Characteristic	Total employed	Number of workers by usual weekly earnings							
		Under $350.00	$350.00 to $499.99	$500.00 to $599.99	$600.00 to $749.99	$750.00 to $999.99	$1,000.00 to $1,199.99	$1,200.00 to $1,999.99	$2,000.00 or more
Age									
Total, 16 years and older............	104,262	7,881	16,496	10,022	14,128	17,822	10,179	18,784	8,951
16 to 24 years............	9,247	2,130	3,270	1,175	1,214	864	305	240	50
16 to 19 years............	1,084	441	407	91	73	41	11	17	3
20 to 24 years............	8,164	1,690	2,863	1,084	1,141	823	293	222	47
25 years and older............	95,015	5,751	13,225	8,847	12,914	16,958	9,875	18,544	8,901
25 to 34 years............	25,081	1,889	4,578	2,870	3,910	4,680	2,448	3,683	1,023
35 to 44 years............	24,303	1,354	3,039	2,051	3,216	4,314	2,503	5,268	2,559
45 to 54 years............	25,100	1,309	3,106	2,143	3,239	4,464	2,648	5,294	2,898
55 to 64 years............	17,066	848	2,024	1,453	2,135	2,983	1,981	3,649	1,993
65 years and older............	3,465	351	479	331	414	517	295	650	428
Women, 16 years and older............	46,268	4,345	8,275	5,173	6,800	8,009	4,370	6,866	2,430
16 to 24 years............	4,041	1,089	1,475	496	486	326	101	53	15
16 to 19 years............	453	222	167	24	25	10	3	2	1
20 to 24 years............	3,587	866	1,308	471	462	316	98	50	14
25 years and older............	42,228	3,256	6,800	4,678	6,314	7,684	4,269	6,813	2,415
25 to 34 years............	10,891	961	2,061	1,385	1,841	2,049	1,038	1,288	268
35 to 44 years............	10,480	787	1,553	1,063	1,519	1,891	1,047	1,896	723
45 to 54 years............	11,391	825	1,772	1,204	1,626	2,075	1,161	1,956	772
55 to 64 years............	7,967	503	1,164	854	1,114	1,425	895	1,441	571
65 years and older............	1,498	180	250	172	213	243	127	232	81
Men, 16 years and older............	57,994	3,537	8,221	4,849	7,328	9,813	5,809	11,918	6,521
16 to 24 years............	5,207	1,042	1,795	679	727	539	203	187	34
16 to 19 years............	630	218	240	66	48	31	8	15	2
20 to 24 years............	4,577	823	1,555	613	679	507	195	172	32
25 years and older............	52,787	2,495	6,426	4,170	6,600	9,274	5,606	11,731	6,486
25 to 34 years............	14,190	928	2,517	1,485	2,069	2,631	1,410	2,395	755
35 to 44 years............	13,823	567	1,486	987	1,697	2,422	1,455	3,371	1,837
45 to 54 years............	13,708	484	1,333	939	1,613	2,389	1,487	3,338	2,126
55 to 64 years............	9,100	346	860	599	1,021	1,557	1,086	2,208	1,421
65 years and older............	1,966	171	229	159	200	274	167	418	348
Race and Hispanic or Latino Ethnicity									
White............	82,672	5,746	12,298	7,753	11,180	14,496	8,349	15,362	7,487
Women............	35,619	3,084	6,074	3,928	5,348	6,360	3,488	5,415	1,922
Men............	47,053	2,663	6,224	3,825	5,832	8,136	4,861	9,947	5,566
Black or African American............	12,439	1,457	2,715	1,476	1,878	1,966	950	1,527	469
Women............	6,588	876	1,507	844	954	974	499	726	209
Men............	5,851	581	1,208	632	925	992	451	802	260
Asian............	6,073	387	812	463	629	887	630	1,461	805
Women............	2,698	211	401	248	311	457	281	561	229
Men............	3,376	176	411	215	318	430	349	901	576
Hispanic or Latino ethnicity............	16,859	2,355	4,407	1,961	2,448	2,394	1,040	1,689	566
Women............	6,534	1,129	1,743	774	907	929	385	516	150
Men............	10,325	1,226	2,663	1,187	1,541	1,465	655	1,173	415

Note: Estimates for the race groups shown (White, Black or African American, and Asian) do not sum to totals because data are not presented for all race groups. People of Hispanic or Latino ethnicity may be of any race; estimates for the race groups include Hispanics.
Source: U.S. Bureau of Labor Statistics.

Table 7. Median usual weekly earnings of full-time wage and salary workers, by marital status and presence and age of own children under 18 years old, 2013 annual averages

Characteristic	Number of workers (in thousands)	Median weekly earnings	Standard error of median
Women			
Total, all marital statuses...	46,268	$706	$3
With children under 18 years old....................................	16,470	701	5
With children 6 to 17, none younger.........................	9,967	720	6
With children under 6 years old................................	6,503	674	7
With no children under 18 years old...............................	29,798	708	3
Total, married, spouse present.......................................	23,915	768	3
With children under 18 years old....................................	10,855	781	6
With children 6 to 17, none younger.........................	6,529	771	6
With children under 6 years old................................	4,326	800	12
With no children under 18 years old...............................	13,060	760	4
Total, other marital statuses[1].......................................	22,353	630	3
With children under 18 years old....................................	5,615	575	5
With children 6 to 17, none younger.........................	3,438	617	5
With children under 6 years old................................	2,176	496	6
With no children under 18 years old...............................	16,738	659	4
Men			
Total, all marital statuses...	57,994	860	3
With children under 18 years old....................................	21,293	950	5
With children 6 to 17, none younger.........................	11,584	1,005	9
With children under 6 years old................................	9,710	890	8
With no children under 18 years old...............................	36,701	804	4
Total, married, spouse present.......................................	34,695	985	5
With children under 18 years old....................................	18,799	990	6
With children 6 to 17, none younger.........................	10,335	1,038	12
With children under 6 years old................................	8,464	942	8
With no children under 18 years old...............................	15,896	979	6
Total, other marital statuses[1].......................................	23,299	687	4
With children under 18 years old....................................	2,495	692	10
With children 6 to 17, none younger.........................	1,249	796	20
With children under 6 years old................................	1,245	598	9
With no children under 18 years old...............................	20,805	686	4

[1] Includes never-married, divorced, separated, and widowed persons.

Note: Children refer to "own" children and include sons, daughters, stepchildren, and adopted children. Excluded are other related children such as grandchildren, nieces, nephews, and cousins, as well as unrelated children.
Source: U.S. Bureau of Labor Statistics.

Table 8. Median hourly earnings of wage and salary workers paid hourly rates, by selected characteristics, 2013 annual averages

Characteristic	Total			Women			Men			Women's earnings as a percentage of men's
	Number of workers (in thousands)	Median hourly earnings	Standard error of median	Number of workers (in thousands)	Median hourly earnings	Standard error of median	Number of workers (in thousands)	Median hourly earnings	Standard error of median	
Age										
Total, 16 years and older....................	75,948	$12.93	$0.03	38,404	$12.12	$0.02	37,544	$14.00	$0.04	86.6
16 to 24 years.............................	15,110	9.16	0.02	7,552	8.93	0.03	7,558	9.67	0.07	92.3
16 to 19 years.........................	4,089	8.19	0.02	2,115	8.09	0.02	1,975	8.37	0.05	96.7
20 to 24 years.........................	11,021	9.83	0.02	5,437	9.40	0.08	5,584	10.00	0.03	94.0
25 years and older.......................	60,838	14.50	0.06	30,852	13.36	0.06	29,985	15.27	0.07	87.5
25 to 34 years.........................	17,607	12.88	0.05	8,326	12.23	0.07	9,281	13.42	0.14	91.1
35 to 44 years.........................	14,195	14.98	0.04	7,082	13.77	0.12	7,112	16.21	0.16	84.9
45 to 54 years.........................	15,097	15.17	0.05	7,916	13.94	0.07	7,181	17.17	0.14	81.2
55 to 64 years.........................	10,713	15.62	0.15	5,798	14.53	0.18	4,915	17.28	0.22	84.1
65 years and older.....................	3,227	12.47	0.20	1,731	12.22	0.14	1,496	12.88	0.22	94.9
Race and Hispanic or Latino Ethnicity										
White..	59,515	13.15	0.04	29,569	12.21	0.04	29,947	14.24	0.09	85.7
Black or African American....................	10,233	11.90	0.04	5,643	11.54	0.13	4,590	12.16	0.06	94.9
Asian..	3,495	13.62	0.27	1,888	13.04	0.18	1,606	14.24	0.28	91.6
Hispanic or Latino ethnicity..................	14,706	11.25	0.09	6,341	10.49	0.11	8,365	11.99	0.05	87.5
Marital Status										
Never married.................................	28,651	10.23	0.03	13,697	10.04	0.02	14,954	10.83	0.05	92.7
Married, spouse present.....................	34,479	15.10	0.03	16,965	13.99	0.05	17,514	16.55	0.12	84.5
Other marital status..........................	12,818	13.65	0.10	7,742	12.77	0.09	5,076	15.07	0.07	84.7
Divorced..................................	8,133	14.50	0.16	4,813	13.29	0.13	3,320	16.04	0.14	82.9
Separated.................................	3,236	12.07	0.07	1,799	11.53	0.16	1,437	13.09	0.20	88.1
Widowed..................................	1,449	12.78	0.19	1,130	12.65	0.24	319	13.22	0.49	95.7
Union Affiliation[1]										
Members of unions[2].........................	8,641	18.58	0.19	3,383	16.36	0.22	5,258	20.09	0.08	81.4
Represented by unions[3].....................	9,440	18.34	0.16	3,781	16.23	0.19	5,659	20.02	0.08	81.1
Not represented by a union..................	66,508	12.21	0.03	34,624	11.89	0.02	31,884	13.02	0.05	91.3
Educational Attainment										
Total, 25 years and older....................	60,838	14.50	0.06	30,852	13.36	0.06	29,985	15.27	0.07	87.5
Less than a high school diploma..........	6,821	10.51	0.11	2,586	9.68	0.10	4,235	11.76	0.10	82.3
High school graduates, no college........	21,374	13.73	0.07	9,846	12.07	0.04	11,528	15.15	0.04	79.7
Some college or associate degree........	20,084	14.92	0.04	10,993	13.79	0.07	9,092	16.47	0.16	83.7
Bachelor's degree and higher..............	12,558	19.02	0.13	7,428	18.52	0.22	5,131	19.78	0.22	93.6

[1] Differences in earnings levels between workers with and without union affiliation reflect a variety of factors in addition to coverage by a collective bargaining agreement, including the distribution of workers by occupation, industry, and geographic region.

[2] Data refer to members of a labor union or an employee association similar to a union.

[3] Data refer to both union members and workers who report no union affiliation but whose jobs are covered by a union or an employee association contract.

Note: Estimates for the race groups shown (White, Black or African American, and Asian) do not sum to totals because data are not presented for all race groups. People of Hispanic or Latino ethnicity may be of any race; estimates for the race groups include Hispanics.
Source: U.S. Bureau of Labor Statistics.

Table 9. Distribution of wage and salary workers paid hourly rates, by hourly earnings and selected demographic characteristics, 2013 annual averages

[In thousands]

Characteristic	Total employed	Number of workers by hourly earnings						
		Under $6.00	$6.00 to $7.99	$8.00 to $9.99	$10.00 to $11.99	$12.00 to $14.99	$15.00 to $19.99	$20.00 or more
Age								
Total, 16 years and older..............................	75,948	1,202	4,694	13,800	12,195	12,795	14,201	17,060
16 to 24 years.......................................	15,110	522	2,527	5,500	3,041	1,902	1,201	418
16 to 19 years...................................	4,089	176	1,294	1,713	554	224	93	35
20 to 24 years...................................	11,021	346	1,233	3,787	2,487	1,678	1,107	383
25 years and older..................................	60,838	680	2,167	8,300	9,154	10,894	13,001	16,643
25 to 34 years...................................	17,607	354	774	3,006	3,103	3,442	3,479	3,449
35 to 44 years...................................	14,195	141	471	1,797	2,026	2,369	3,161	4,229
45 to 54 years...................................	15,097	124	431	1,761	2,014	2,621	3,444	4,701
55 to 64 years...................................	10,713	36	287	1,170	1,387	1,916	2,322	3,594
65 years and older...............................	3,227	24	204	566	624	545	594	669
Women, 16 years and older..........................	38,404	842	2,782	7,909	6,362	6,797	6,623	7,089
16 to 24 years.......................................	7,552	371	1,412	2,897	1,412	834	448	177
16 to 19 years...................................	2,115	117	723	900	242	91	30	10
20 to 24 years...................................	5,437	253	688	1,997	1,170	744	418	167
25 years and older..................................	30,852	472	1,371	5,012	4,949	5,963	6,175	6,911
25 to 34 years...................................	8,326	236	432	1,602	1,468	1,656	1,514	1,417
35 to 44 years...................................	7,082	99	310	1,129	1,110	1,295	1,429	1,711
45 to 54 years...................................	7,916	94	310	1,185	1,198	1,557	1,723	1,848
55 to 64 years...................................	5,798	24	199	766	846	1,153	1,206	1,605
65 years and older...............................	1,731	18	120	330	327	302	304	330
Men, 16 years and older.............................	37,544	360	1,912	5,891	5,833	5,998	7,578	9,972
16 to 24 years.......................................	7,558	152	1,115	2,603	1,628	1,067	752	240
16 to 19 years...................................	1,975	59	571	813	312	133	63	25
20 to 24 years...................................	5,584	93	545	1,790	1,317	934	690	216
25 years and older..................................	29,985	208	797	3,289	4,205	4,931	6,826	9,731
25 to 34 years...................................	9,281	118	341	1,404	1,635	1,786	1,965	2,032
35 to 44 years...................................	7,112	42	162	668	916	1,074	1,733	2,518
45 to 54 years...................................	7,181	30	121	575	816	1,064	1,721	2,854
55 to 64 years...................................	4,915	12	89	405	541	764	1,116	1,989
65 years and older...............................	1,496	6	84	236	297	243	291	339
Race and Hispanic or Latino Ethnicity								
White...	59,515	994	3,524	10,393	9,279	9,990	11,276	14,058
Women..	29,569	706	2,092	5,873	4,829	5,223	5,143	5,704
Men...	29,947	289	1,431	4,521	4,450	4,767	6,134	8,355
Black or African American.............................	10,233	117	822	2,193	1,869	1,778	1,878	1,575
Women..	5,643	75	492	1,353	997	1,027	963	736
Men...	4,590	42	330	841	872	752	915	839
Asian...	3,495	36	179	603	561	567	600	949
Women..	1,888	23	95	353	308	319	329	461
Men...	1,606	13	83	250	253	247	271	488
Hispanic or Latino ethnicity............................	14,706	192	982	3,605	2,896	2,588	2,393	2,049
Women..	6,341	109	573	1,844	1,194	1,104	869	647
Men...	8,365	83	409	1,762	1,702	1,484	1,524	1,402

Note: Estimates for the race groups shown (White, Black or African American, and Asian) do not sum to totals because data are not presented for all race groups. People of Hispanic or Latino ethnicity may be of any race; estimates for the race groups include Hispanics.

Source: U.S. Bureau of Labor Statistics.

Table 10. Wage and salary workers paid hourly rates with earnings at or below the prevailing federal minimum wage, by selected demographic characteristics, 2013 annual averages

[Numbers in thousands]

Characteristic	Workers paid hourly rates				
	Total	Below prevailing federal minimum wage	At prevailing federal minimum wage	Total at or below prevailing federal minimum wage	
				Number	Percentage of workers paid hourly rates
Age					
Total, 16 years and older...............	75,948	1,768	1,532	3,301	4.3
16 to 24 years...............	15,110	808	855	1,663	11.0
16 to 19 years...............	4,089	321	476	797	19.5
20 to 24 years...............	11,021	487	379	866	7.9
25 years and older...............	60,838	961	677	1,638	2.7
25 to 34 years...............	17,607	454	249	704	4.0
35 to 44 years...............	14,195	211	144	355	2.5
45 to 54 years...............	15,097	179	135	314	2.1
55 to 64 years...............	10,713	66	89	155	1.4
65 years and older...............	3,227	51	60	111	3.4
Women, 16 years and older...............	38,404	1,148	910	2,058	5.4
16 to 24 years...............	7,552	534	473	1,007	13.3
16 to 19 years...............	2,115	194	272	466	22.0
20 to 24 years...............	5,437	340	201	541	10.0
25 years and older...............	30,852	614	437	1,051	3.4
25 to 34 years...............	8,326	278	140	418	5.0
35 to 44 years...............	7,082	139	100	239	3.4
45 to 54 years...............	7,916	132	99	231	2.9
55 to 64 years...............	5,798	40	59	99	1.7
65 years and older...............	1,731	25	39	64	3.7
Men, 16 years and older...............	37,544	621	622	1,243	3.3
16 to 24 years...............	7,558	273	382	656	8.7
16 to 19 years...............	1,975	127	205	331	16.8
20 to 24 years...............	5,584	147	178	324	5.8
25 years and older...............	29,985	347	240	587	2.0
25 to 34 years...............	9,281	177	109	286	3.1
35 to 44 years...............	7,112	72	44	116	1.6
45 to 54 years...............	7,181	47	36	83	1.2
55 to 64 years...............	4,915	26	29	56	1.1
65 years and older...............	1,496	26	21	47	3.1
Race and Hispanic or Latino Ethnicity					
White...............	59,515	1,394	1,160	2,554	4.3
Women...............	29,569	914	691	1,605	5.4
Men...............	29,947	480	470	949	3.2
Black or African American...............	10,233	224	276	500	4.9
Women...............	5,643	137	155	292	5.2
Men...............	4,590	87	121	209	4.5
Asian...............	3,495	71	43	114	3.3
Women...............	1,888	45	25	70	3.7
Men...............	1,606	26	18	44	2.7
Hispanic or Latino ethnicity...............	14,706	325	318	644	4.4
Women...............	6,341	168	195	363	5.7
Men...............	8,365	157	123	281	3.4
Full- and Part-time Status[1]					
Full-time workers...............	55,387	726	447	1,173	2.1
Women...............	25,078	435	263	698	2.8
Men...............	30,309	291	184	475	1.6
Part-time workers...............	20,453	1,040	1,085	2,125	10.4
Women...............	13,265	711	648	1,359	10.2
Men...............	7,188	328	438	766	10.7

[1] The distinction between full- and part-time workers is based on hours usually worked. These data do not sum to totals because full- or part-time status on the principal job is not identifiable for a small number of multiple jobholders.

Note: See the technical notes section for information about the federal minimum wage level and estimating the number of minimum wage workers. Estimates for the race groups shown (White, Black or African American, and Asian) do not sum to totals because data are not presented for all race groups. People of Hispanic or Latino ethnicity may be of any race; estimates for the race groups include Hispanics.

Source: U.S. Bureau of Labor Statistics.

Table 11. Wage and salary workers paid hourly rates with earnings at or below the prevailing federal minimum wage, 1979-2013 annual averages
[Numbers in thousands]

Year	Total wage and salary workers	Workers paid hourly rates					
		Total	Percentage of total wage and salary workers	Below prevailing federal minimum wage[1]	At prevailing federal minimum wage[1]	Total at or below prevailing federal minimum wage	
						Number	Percentage of workers paid hourly rates
Total							
1979	87,529	51,721	59.1	2,916	3,997	6,912	13.4
1980	87,644	51,335	58.6	3,087	4,686	7,773	15.1
1981	88,516	51,869	58.6	3,513	4,311	7,824	15.1
1982	87,368	50,846	58.2	2,348	4,148	6,496	12.8
1983	88,290	51,820	58.7	2,077	4,261	6,338	12.2
1984	92,194	54,143	58.7	1,838	4,125	5,963	11.0
1985	94,521	55,762	59.0	1,639	3,899	5,538	9.9
1986	96,903	57,529	59.4	1,599	3,461	5,060	8.8
1987	99,303	59,552	60.0	1,468	3,229	4,698	7.9
1988	101,407	60,878	60.0	1,319	2,608	3,927	6.5
1989	103,480	62,389	60.3	1,372	1,790	3,162	5.1
1990	104,876	63,172	60.2	2,132	1,096	3,228	5.1
1991	103,723	62,627	60.4	2,377	2,906	5,283	8.4
1992	104,668	63,610	60.8	1,939	2,982	4,921	7.7
1993	106,101	64,274	60.6	1,707	2,625	4,332	6.7
1994	107,989	66,549	61.6	1,995	2,132	4,128	6.2
1995	110,038	68,354	62.1	1,699	1,956	3,656	5.3
1996	111,960	69,255	61.9	1,863	1,861	3,724	5.4
1997	114,533	70,735	61.8	2,990	1,764	4,754	6.7
1998	116,730	71,440	61.2	2,834	1,593	4,427	6.2
1999	118,963	72,306	60.8	2,194	1,146	3,340	4.6
2000	122,089	73,496	60.2	1,752	898	2,650	3.6
2001	122,229	73,392	60.0	1,518	656	2,174	3.0
2002	121,826	72,508	59.5	1,579	567	2,146	3.0
2003	122,358	72,946	59.6	1,555	545	2,100	2.9
2004	123,554	73,939	59.8	1,483	520	2,003	2.7
2005	125,889	75,609	60.1	1,403	479	1,882	2.5
2006	128,237	76,514	59.7	1,283	409	1,692	2.2
2007	129,767	75,873	58.5	1,462	267	1,729	2.3
2008	129,377	75,305	58.2	1,940	286	2,226	3.0
2009	124,490	72,611	58.3	2,592	980	3,572	4.9
2010	124,073	72,902	58.8	2,541	1,820	4,361	6.0
2011	125,187	73,926	59.1	2,152	1,677	3,829	5.2
2012	127,577	75,276	59.0	1,984	1,566	3,550	4.7
2013	129,110	75,948	58.8	1,768	1,532	3,301	4.3
Women							
1979	38,129	23,329	61.2	2,070	2,644	4,714	20.2
1980	38,944	23,626	60.7	2,104	2,990	5,095	21.6
1981	39,672	24,294	61.2	2,394	2,778	5,172	21.3
1982	39,777	24,365	61.3	1,651	2,561	4,212	17.3
1983	40,433	24,989	61.8	1,492	2,603	4,095	16.4
1984	42,172	26,003	61.7	1,348	2,499	3,847	14.8
1985	43,506	26,869	61.8	1,198	2,356	3,554	13.2
1986	44,961	27,863	62.0	1,192	2,125	3,317	11.9
1987	46,365	29,078	62.7	1,105	1,946	3,051	10.5
1988	47,495	29,820	62.8	1,008	1,542	2,550	8.6
1989	48,691	30,702	63.1	994	1,056	2,050	6.7
1990	49,323	31,069	63.0	1,420	711	2,131	6.9
1991	49,105	30,988	63.1	1,582	1,792	3,374	10.9
1992	49,842	31,454	63.1	1,286	1,751	3,036	9.7
1993	50,626	31,937	63.1	1,133	1,534	2,667	8.4
1994	51,419	33,021	64.2	1,322	1,241	2,563	7.8
1995	52,369	33,934	64.8	1,157	1,161	2,318	6.8
1996	53,488	34,418	64.3	1,244	1,106	2,350	6.8
1997	54,708	35,214	64.4	1,843	1,092	2,935	8.3
1998	55,757	35,680	64.0	1,794	965	2,760	7.7

Table 11. Wage and salary workers paid hourly rates with earnings at or below the prevailing federal minimum wage, 1979-2013 annual averages — Continued

[Numbers in thousands]

Year	Total wage and salary workers	Workers paid hourly rates					
		Total	Percentage of total wage and salary workers	Below prevailing federal minimum wage[1]	At prevailing federal minimum wage[1]	Total at or below prevailing federal minimum wage	
						Number	Percentage of workers paid hourly rates
1999.	57,050	36,233	63.5	1,426	700	2,126	5.9
2000.	58,427	36,777	62.9	1,170	579	1,749	4.8
2001.	58,582	36,848	62.9	1,021	409	1,430	3.9
2002.	58,555	36,508	62.3	997	350	1,347	3.7
2003.	59,122	37,093	62.7	1,062	332	1,394	3.8
2004.	59,408	37,133	62.5	1,013	310	1,323	3.6
2005.	60,423	37,957	62.8	944	290	1,234	3.3
2006.	61,426	38,321	62.4	861	263	1,124	2.9
2007.	62,299	38,082	61.1	1,002	181	1,183	3.1
2008.	62,532	37,972	60.7	1,302	196	1,498	3.9
2009.	60,951	37,426	61.4	1,603	612	2,215	5.9
2010.	60,542	37,404	61.8	1,598	1,151	2,749	7.3
2011.	60,502	37,469	61.9	1,366	1,029	2,395	6.4
2012.	61,679	38,163	61.9	1,288	999	2,287	6.0
2013.	62,316	38,404	61.6	1,148	910	2,058	5.4
Men							
1979.	49,400	28,392	57.5	846	1,353	2,199	7.7
1980.	48,700	27,709	56.9	983	1,696	2,678	9.7
1981.	48,844	27,576	56.5	1,119	1,533	2,652	9.6
1982.	47,591	26,481	55.6	697	1,587	2,284	8.6
1983.	47,856	26,831	56.1	585	1,658	2,243	8.4
1984.	50,022	28,140	56.3	490	1,626	2,116	7.5
1985.	51,015	28,893	56.6	440	1,544	1,984	6.9
1986.	51,942	29,666	57.1	408	1,336	1,743	5.9
1987.	52,938	30,474	57.6	364	1,283	1,647	5.4
1988.	53,912	31,058	57.6	311	1,066	1,377	4.4
1989.	54,789	31,687	57.8	379	733	1,112	3.5
1990.	55,553	32,104	57.8	712	385	1,097	3.4
1991.	54,618	31,639	57.9	795	1,114	1,909	6.0
1992.	54,826	32,155	58.6	653	1,231	1,885	5.9
1993.	55,475	32,337	58.3	573	1,091	1,664	5.1
1994.	56,570	33,528	59.3	674	891	1,565	4.7
1995.	57,669	34,420	59.7	542	796	1,338	3.9
1996.	58,473	34,838	59.6	619	755	1,374	3.9
1997.	59,825	35,521	59.4	1,147	673	1,820	5.1
1998.	60,973	35,761	58.7	1,039	628	1,667	4.7
1999.	61,914	36,073	58.3	768	446	1,214	3.4
2000.	63,662	36,720	57.7	582	319	901	2.5
2001.	63,647	36,544	57.4	497	247	744	2.0
2002.	63,272	36,000	56.9	582	217	799	2.2
2003.	63,236	35,853	56.7	493	213	706	2.0
2004.	64,145	36,806	57.4	470	210	680	1.8
2005.	65,466	37,652	57.5	459	189	648	1.7
2006.	66,811	38,193	57.2	422	146	568	1.5
2007.	67,468	37,790	56.0	460	86	546	1.4
2008.	66,846	37,334	55.9	638	90	728	1.9
2009.	63,539	35,185	55.4	990	368	1,358	3.9
2010.	63,531	35,498	55.9	943	669	1,612	4.5
2011.	64,686	36,457	56.4	785	648	1,433	3.9
2012.	65,898	37,113	56.3	696	567	1,263	3.4
2013.	66,794	37,544	56.2	621	622	1,243	3.3

[1] Data for 1990-91, 1996-97, and 2007-09 reflect changes in the minimum wage that took place in those years.

Note: The comparability of historical labor force data has been affected at various times by methodological and other changes in the Current Population Survey (CPS). Information about historical comparability is online at www.bls.gov/cps/documentation.htm#comp. See the technical notes section for information about the federal minimum wage level and estimating the number of minimum wage workers.

Source: U.S. Bureau of Labor Statistics.

Table 12. Women's earnings as a percentage of men's, by age, for full-time wage and salary workers, 1979-2013

Year	Total, 16 years and older	16 to 24 years			25 years and older					
		Total	16 to 19 years	20 to 24 years	Total	25 to 34 years	35 to 44 years	45 to 54 years	55 to 64 years	65 years and older
1979.............................	62.3	78.6	85.2	76.3	62.1	67.5	58.3	56.8	60.6	77.6
1980.............................	64.2	80.3	89.5	78.1	62.8	69.4	58.3	56.9	59.4	76.4
1981.............................	64.4	82.6	91.7	80.6	62.6	70.3	59.9	56.8	58.9	71.1
1982.............................	65.7	85.3	92.9	82.4	64.9	72.1	61.1	60.1	61.4	70.3
1983.............................	66.5	88.8	94.0	85.5	65.8	73.3	61.5	59.5	61.8	68.8
1984.............................	67.6	87.9	93.1	85.2	67.1	74.6	62.0	59.4	61.5	66.8
1985.............................	68.1	87.6	90.7	85.7	66.8	75.1	63.0	59.7	61.0	65.9
1986.............................	69.5	89.0	91.4	87.5	66.5	76.1	63.9	60.9	61.2	71.5
1987.............................	69.8	88.3	87.8	88.0	67.3	76.7	66.1	62.3	62.2	68.7
1988.............................	70.2	89.7	89.8	90.0	68.8	77.7	68.5	61.7	62.3	70.9
1989.............................	70.1	90.8	94.3	89.7	70.2	78.3	68.3	62.7	63.9	74.3
1990.............................	71.9	90.1	90.8	90.3	72.1	79.3	69.6	63.8	63.7	74.4
1991.............................	74.2	93.3	93.6	93.3	74.0	81.0	70.7	65.0	64.5	68.3
1992.............................	75.8	94.0	94.0	94.3	74.6	82.0	71.9	65.8	64.9	77.9
1993.............................	77.1	94.8	92.8	95.4	74.8	83.0	73.0	67.4	67.4	74.3
1994.............................	76.4	93.9	92.5	94.5	73.1	82.9	72.6	67.1	66.0	76.2
1995.............................	75.5	90.8	88.1	92.4	72.8	82.2	72.6	67.7	64.7	80.0
1996.............................	75.0	92.5	88.8	92.8	74.1	83.2	73.3	68.9	65.3	70.0
1997.............................	74.4	92.1	91.6	90.5	75.1	82.9	74.0	69.4	64.7	77.0
1998.............................	76.3	91.3	88.6	89.4	75.9	82.9	73.6	70.5	68.1	72.6
1999.............................	76.5	91.0	91.4	90.5	74.4	81.5	71.7	70.0	67.9	78.7
2000.............................	76.9	91.7	92.5	92.7	74.5	82.4	71.6	73.2	69.1	75.1
2001.............................	76.4	90.3	90.3	91.9	75.4	83.0	72.5	73.5	70.5	69.0
2002.............................	77.9	93.9	94.6	93.9	77.6	84.5	75.2	74.6	71.6	73.8
2003.............................	79.4	93.2	93.1	93.9	78.5	86.9	76.1	73.0	72.7	71.1
2004.............................	80.4	93.8	92.1	93.8	78.6	87.8	75.6	72.9	73.0	74.6
2005.............................	81.0	93.2	92.1	93.8	79.4	89.0	75.5	75.5	74.7	76.4
2006.............................	80.8	94.5	87.6	94.9	78.7	88.2	77.2	73.5	72.9	77.5
2007.............................	80.2	92.3	89.1	90.3	78.5	86.9	76.5	74.5	72.8	77.8
2008.............................	79.9	91.1	87.3	92.5	78.2	88.5	74.5	74.9	75.4	74.8
2009.............................	80.2	92.6	90.7	92.9	78.7	88.7	77.4	73.6	75.3	76.1
2010.............................	81.2	95.3	94.6	93.8	80.5	90.8	79.9	76.5	75.2	75.7
2011.............................	82.2	92.5	88.6	93.2	81.0	92.3	78.5	76.0	75.1	80.9
2012.............................	80.9	88.9	88.5	89.0	79.9	90.2	78.1	75.1	76.2	77.6
2013.............................	82.1	88.3	89.7	89.8	81.1	89.4	80.2	76.6	77.1	73.7

Note: The comparability of historical labor force data has been affected at various times by methodological and other changes in the Current Population Survey (CPS). Information about historical comparability is online at www.bls.gov/cps/documentation.htm#comp. The women's-to-men's earnings ratios shown here are calculated from the current-dollar median usual weekly earnings of full-time wage and salary workers in table 22.
Source: U.S. Bureau of Labor Statistics.

Table 13. Women's earnings as a percentage of men's, by race and Hispanic or Latino ethnicity, for full-time wage and salary workers, 1979-2013

Year	Total, 16 years and older	White	Black or African American	Asian	Hispanic or Latino ethnicity
1979..	62.3	61.7	74.4	–	71.7
1980..	64.2	63.4	75.8	–	73.5
1981..	64.4	63.1	76.9	–	75.7
1982..	65.7	64.5	78.1	–	75.5
1983..	66.5	65.6	78.9	–	78.5
1984..	67.6	66.8	79.5	–	77.7
1985..	68.1	67.2	82.6	–	77.7
1986..	69.5	67.9	82.8	–	80.6
1987..	69.8	68.2	84.4	–	82.0
1988..	70.2	68.4	82.8	–	84.4
1989..	70.1	69.3	86.5	–	85.4
1990..	71.9	71.5	85.3	–	87.4
1991..	74.2	73.7	86.1	–	90.4
1992..	75.8	75.3	88.2	–	89.1
1993..	77.1	76.5	88.8	–	90.5
1994..	76.4	74.6	86.5	–	88.9
1995..	75.5	73.3	86.4	–	87.1
1996..	75.0	73.8	87.9	–	88.8
1997..	74.4	74.6	86.8	–	85.7
1998..	76.3	76.1	85.5	–	86.4
1999..	76.5	75.7	83.8	–	85.7
2000..	76.9	75.8	84.1	79.9	87.8
2001..	76.4	75.8	85.8	76.9	88.2
2002..	77.9	77.9	90.3	74.9	88.0
2003..	79.4	79.3	88.5	77.5	88.4
2004..	80.4	79.8	88.8	76.4	87.3
2005..	81.0	80.2	89.3	80.6	87.7
2006..	80.8	80.0	87.8	79.3	87.1
2007..	80.2	79.4	88.8	78.1	91.0
2008..	79.9	79.3	89.4	78.0	89.6
2009..	80.2	79.2	93.7	81.8	89.5
2010..	81.2	80.5	93.5	82.6	90.7
2011..	82.2	82.1	91.1	77.4	90.7
2012..	80.9	80.8	90.1	73.0	88.0
2013..	82.1	81.7	91.3	77.3	91.1

Note: The comparability of historical labor force data has been affected at various times by methodological and other changes in the Current Population Survey (CPS). Information about historical comparability is online at www.bls.gov/cps/documentation.htm#comp. The women's-to-men's earnings ratios shown here are calculated from the current-dollar median usual weekly earnings of full-time wage and salary workers in table 23. As of 2003, estimates for the race groups shown (White, Black or African American, and Asian) include people who selected that race group only; people who selected more than one race group are not included. Prior to 2003, people who reported more than one race were included in the group they identified as the main race. Asian data for 2000-2002 are for Asians and Pacific Islanders. As of 2003, Asians constitute a separate category. Data for Asians were not tabulated prior to 2000. People of Hispanic or Latino ethnicity may be of any race; estimates for the race groups include Hispanics. Dash indicates data not available.
Source: U.S. Bureau of Labor Statistics.

Table 14. Women's earnings as a percentage of men's, by educational attainment, for full-time wage and salary workers 25 years and older, 1979-2013

Year	Total, 25 years and older	Less than a high school diploma	High school graduates, no college	Some college or associate degree	Bachelor's degree and higher
1979	62.1	60.3	60.1	64.1	66.7
1980	62.8	61.4	61.5	64.5	67.9
1981	62.6	61.2	61.0	65.6	66.9
1982	64.9	62.8	63.1	66.7	68.8
1983	65.8	64.8	63.4	68.2	71.2
1984	67.1	64.9	64.9	68.4	69.4
1985	66.8	64.3	65.8	67.2	70.2
1986	66.5	64.8	66.6	68.0	70.6
1987	67.3	66.0	68.1	69.8	71.4
1988	68.8	66.6	68.2	71.6	71.4
1989	70.2	66.8	67.6	73.3	71.9
1990	72.1	68.8	68.6	72.9	72.2
1991	74.0	71.6	69.8	72.6	73.6
1992	74.6	72.9	70.4	73.3	75.1
1993	74.8	73.9	71.3	73.8	75.8
1994	73.1	75.1	70.8	72.1	76.8
1995	72.8	75.5	70.2	71.6	76.2
1996	74.1	75.1	70.7	73.2	75.2
1997	75.1	75.3	70.7	73.9	75.0
1998	75.9	73.9	70.8	74.0	75.3
1999	74.4	73.4	69.8	73.4	75.7
2000	74.5	74.9	71.1	73.1	74.1
2001	75.4	75.4	72.7	71.9	73.7
2002	77.6	77.2	74.2	74.3	74.2
2003	78.5	76.7	75.5	75.7	73.6
2004	78.6	74.9	75.7	75.8	75.2
2005	79.4	74.9	75.6	76.6	75.7
2006	78.7	76.3	73.7	75.6	75.1
2007	78.5	76.7	74.3	75.2	75.0
2008	78.2	76.1	73.3	75.7	74.3
2009	78.7	76.4	75.7	75.4	73.1
2010	80.5	79.8	76.5	75.5	74.1
2011	81.0	80.9	76.9	76.8	74.9
2012	79.9	76.0	76.3	76.9	73.0
2013	81.1	80.0	78.3	76.6	74.8

Note: The comparability of historical labor force data has been affected at various times by methodological and other changes in the Current Population Survey (CPS). Information about historical comparability is online at www.bls.gov/cps/documentation.htm#comp. The women's-to-men's earnings ratios shown here are calculated from the current-dollar median usual weekly earnings of full-time wage and salary workers 25 years and older in table 24.
Source: U.S. Bureau of Labor Statistics.

Table 15. Women's earnings as a percentage of men's, by age, for wage and salary workers paid hourly rates, 1979-2013

Year	Total, 16 years and older	16 to 24 years			25 years and older					
		Total	16 to 19 years	20 to 24 years	Total	25 to 34 years	35 to 44 years	45 to 54 years	55 to 64 years	65 years and older
1979..	64.1	81.8	95.0	75.9	58.3	63.3	55.8	54.1	56.9	87.6
1980..	64.8	84.1	93.2	77.0	58.7	64.1	54.9	54.4	56.4	89.2
1981..	65.1	86.1	96.7	80.0	60.3	66.7	57.5	54.1	56.2	88.1
1982..	67.3	86.3	97.0	81.8	62.1	67.7	57.1	55.7	59.0	88.1
1983..	69.4	87.2	96.7	84.4	62.9	70.3	57.6	56.7	58.0	87.6
1984..	69.8	86.0	96.5	84.5	63.7	71.1	59.0	56.9	59.5	89.0
1985..	70.0	85.7	96.3	87.2	64.7	72.4	60.3	57.8	60.4	88.8
1986..	70.2	85.8	95.5	86.7	66.0	74.1	61.4	59.0	60.3	91.3
1987..	72.1	85.9	93.9	86.1	67.2	74.3	62.9	61.3	62.0	91.2
1988..	73.8	89.1	94.4	87.2	68.7	75.6	66.1	61.6	62.4	92.8
1989..	75.4	90.7	93.4	86.9	69.8	78.0	67.0	63.4	63.8	87.1
1990..	77.9	91.0	93.8	90.1	71.8	79.4	68.7	64.3	66.2	89.6
1991..	78.6	91.0	97.9	91.7	73.5	80.4	70.4	65.0	68.9	92.6
1992..	80.3	91.3	97.7	92.5	76.0	82.6	73.1	66.1	69.3	92.6
1993..	80.4	91.7	97.1	94.2	77.3	83.6	73.1	67.3	69.0	92.1
1994..	80.6	90.5	97.0	91.2	78.2	85.5	73.4	69.9	70.7	94.0
1995..	80.8	90.9	96.1	89.3	76.1	83.7	72.6	70.8	71.4	94.2
1996..	81.2	92.1	97.0	89.6	78.2	83.1	74.6	72.1	72.4	91.6
1997..	80.8	92.2	96.6	91.2	78.8	82.7	75.7	72.3	70.5	98.1
1998..	81.8	90.3	96.7	89.1	77.9	86.1	77.4	75.0	72.4	93.2
1999..	83.8	92.7	96.8	89.9	79.4	83.9	76.9	72.7	76.4	95.4
2000..	83.8	91.7	93.8	93.0	80.8	88.3	76.3	73.2	76.8	94.7
2001..	85.2	90.5	95.8	89.7	79.2	85.8	75.0	76.1	80.2	90.4
2002..	85.0	92.5	96.9	91.3	82.1	85.1	78.7	77.6	80.8	89.3
2003..	84.8	93.2	97.6	91.0	83.1	87.5	79.1	79.0	78.4	90.3
2004..	84.6	93.9	95.9	91.7	81.7	88.3	78.4	79.1	79.6	92.5
2005..	84.8	92.6	96.0	92.4	83.2	89.2	79.6	80.2	80.2	97.8
2006..	84.0	90.9	95.7	90.5	83.2	87.6	80.0	76.4	80.6	93.0
2007..	84.8	89.3	95.4	90.4	81.7	87.4	81.5	79.6	79.2	92.2
2008..	85.4	91.2	96.6	91.6	83.0	87.0	80.5	78.2	81.8	91.6
2009..	85.5	93.1	97.1	92.0	84.7	90.6	80.7	77.0	84.5	92.6
2010..	86.0	93.6	97.8	91.7	85.6	91.9	82.9	79.9	83.2	93.8
2011..	86.8	94.6	97.5	92.5	86.7	92.0	83.8	81.5	82.2	91.5
2012..	86.4	93.0	97.9	92.0	86.8	91.5	83.9	81.2	83.1	90.9
2013..	86.6	92.3	96.7	94.0	87.5	91.1	84.9	81.2	84.1	94.9

Note: The comparability of historical labor force data has been affected at various times by methodological and other changes in the Current Population Survey (CPS). Information on historical comparability is online at www.bls.gov/cps/documentation.htm#comp. The women's-to-men's earnings ratios shown here are calculated from the current-dollar median hourly earnings of workers paid hourly rates in table 25.
Source: U.S. Bureau of Labor Statistics.

Table 16. Women's earnings as a percentage of men's, by race and Hispanic or Latino ethnicity, for wage and salary workers paid hourly rates, 1979-2013

Year	Total, 16 years and older	White	Black or African American	Asian	Hispanic or Latino ethnicity
1979................	64.1	62.5	72.6	–	71.8
1980................	64.8	63.6	74.9	–	75.1
1981................	65.1	63.8	72.1	–	76.4
1982................	67.3	66.0	75.2	–	75.6
1983................	69.4	68.0	79.2	–	76.1
1984................	69.8	68.6	79.1	–	77.0
1985................	70.0	67.8	82.0	–	79.4
1986................	70.2	68.8	78.7	–	80.8
1987................	72.1	70.9	80.1	–	80.2
1988................	73.8	72.7	80.8	–	81.1
1989................	75.4	74.0	83.2	–	83.0
1990................	77.9	75.6	84.5	–	86.1
1991................	78.6	76.6	86.5	–	86.9
1992................	80.3	78.6	87.1	–	88.3
1993................	80.4	78.9	89.6	–	88.6
1994................	80.6	79.7	87.5	–	89.3
1995................	80.8	78.4	87.3	–	90.9
1996................	81.2	79.6	88.0	–	88.8
1997................	80.8	80.3	87.5	–	86.3
1998................	81.8	81.8	86.9	–	87.6
1999................	83.8	82.3	83.2	–	86.6
2000................	83.8	83.0	88.8	90.5	87.3
2001................	85.2	83.8	89.9	85.1	85.6
2002................	85.0	83.8	92.3	91.7	86.1
2003................	84.8	84.0	91.7	89.8	88.5
2004................	84.6	84.0	91.3	88.8	90.2
2005................	84.8	84.2	91.1	91.3	90.1
2006................	84.0	83.6	88.5	90.7	87.6
2007................	84.8	83.7	90.3	89.5	88.5
2008................	85.4	84.5	89.9	87.3	85.1
2009................	85.5	84.8	89.7	90.4	84.6
2010................	86.0	85.0	92.1	88.0	86.2
2011................	86.8	85.9	93.5	89.8	86.8
2012................	86.4	85.3	92.0	90.1	85.4
2013................	86.6	85.7	94.9	91.6	87.5

Note: The comparability of historical labor force data has been affected at various times by methodological and other changes in the Current Population Survey (CPS). Information about historical comparability is online at www.bls.gov/cps/documentation.htm#comp. The women's-to-men's earnings ratios shown here are calculated from the current-dollar median hourly earnings of wage and salary workers paid hourly rates in table 26. As of 2003, estimates for the race groups shown (White, Black or African American, and Asian) include people who selected that race group only; people who selected more than one race group are not included. Prior to 2003, people who reported more than one race were included in the group they identified as the main race. Asian data for 2000-2002 are for Asians and Pacific Islanders. As of 2003, Asians constitute a separate category. Data for Asians were not tabulated prior to 2000. People of Hispanic or Latino ethnicity may be of any race; estimates for the race groups include Hispanics. Dash indicates data not available.
Source: U.S. Bureau of Labor Statistics.

Table 17. Inflation-adjusted median usual weekly earnings, by age, for full-time wage and salary workers, 1979-2013 annual averages
[In constant 2013 dollars]

Year	Total, 16 years and older	16 to 24 years			25 years and older					
		Total	16 to 19 years	20 to 24 years	Total	25 to 34 years	35 to 44 years	45 to 54 years	55 to 64 years	65 years and older
Total										
1979	$722	$515	$431	$557	$793	$763	$838	$826	$784	$593
1980	704	503	414	538	769	742	812	801	766	546
1981	698	491	396	523	757	727	801	786	759	545
1982	701	483	381	510	759	722	821	800	754	587
1983	696	469	364	496	762	713	822	816	769	580
1984	697	464	361	494	774	716	831	823	782	581
1985	711	463	360	496	783	721	839	826	787	614
1986	728	471	361	503	793	730	850	844	805	604
1987	733	476	365	508	790	731	853	841	794	608
1988	728	471	371	503	783	724	851	856	792	611
1989	724	470	370	501	775	715	857	857	782	606
1990	712	465	361	492	775	703	839	845	789	592
1991	710	462	355	485	778	692	830	845	782	635
1992	715	449	345	472	779	686	818	849	785	615
1993	729	448	340	471	779	692	821	860	781	624
1994	726	445	344	467	778	683	835	880	779	597
1995	727	443	351	464	774	684	835	883	780	590
1996	725	441	355	462	769	685	827	879	791	568
1997	728	443	365	465	781	696	838	878	808	569
1998	746	455	382	484	816	716	852	884	845	578
1999	768	477	393	508	828	724	855	912	845	565
2000	779	488	402	518	824	743	846	905	839	627
2001	784	493	401	518	829	758	864	912	839	642
2002	788	494	395	517	837	766	865	915	873	650
2003	785	490	394	509	838	752	870	915	896	653
2004	787	481	381	501	842	745	879	916	894	691
2005	777	474	379	490	831	728	872	893	885	679
2006	775	472	374	488	829	717	864	893	883	673
2007	781	476	379	506	829	722	864	888	902	680
2008	781	479	378	505	824	721	870	890	893	697
2009	802	480	374	504	840	736	887	910	913	743
2010	798	462	371	485	835	729	880	902	919	731
2011	783	455	364	473	825	717	866	896	912	768
2012	779	450	361	471	827	717	870	890	910	768
2013	776	454	373	472	827	708	874	883	904	801
Women										
1979	$545	$461	$395	$482	$584	$596	$587	$575	$566	$509
1980	540	449	390	470	573	586	575	562	551	470
1981	538	442	378	469	572	587	585	553	545	464
1982	555	445	367	466	592	599	599	585	568	490
1983	560	440	351	460	596	604	604	587	571	471
1984	566	434	346	455	605	609	624	596	577	468
1985	572	436	343	457	612	612	634	603	589	500
1986	590	444	345	469	625	621	647	625	600	519
1987	594	445	337	475	629	620	661	635	604	512
1988	595	444	348	474	633	618	669	641	599	529
1989	595	446	358	472	637	617	672	648	604	530
1990	598	439	342	465	637	615	674	651	601	518
1991	610	443	342	467	645	618	678	663	605	532
1992	618	434	333	455	650	621	680	678	611	533
1993	624	433	325	459	659	627	690	698	627	532
1994	621	429	328	451	655	617	697	700	619	523
1995	616	417	326	442	649	612	687	704	612	536

Table 17. Inflation-adjusted median usual weekly earnings, by age, for full-time wage and salary workers, 1979-2013 annual averages — Continued
[In constant 2013 dollars]

Year	Total, 16 years and older	16 to 24 years			25 years and older					
		Total	16 to 19 years	20 to 24 years	Total	25 to 34 years	35 to 44 years	45 to 54 years	55 to 64 years	65 years and older
1996...........................	618	420	330	441	657	614	685	712	621	494
1997...........................	624	423	347	443	669	618	698	716	627	504
1998...........................	650	435	355	455	692	643	710	736	679	499
1999...........................	662	453	372	480	695	657	703	747	688	517
2000...........................	667	465	383	495	698	667	705	763	687	530
2001...........................	674	464	379	493	714	674	720	772	705	513
2002...........................	685	475	382	499	736	687	740	780	744	557
2003...........................	699	470	378	490	739	691	747	771	761	551
2004...........................	707	462	361	482	739	692	750	771	758	589
2005...........................	698	455	363	473	730	684	741	768	763	587
2006...........................	693	456	352	477	724	673	745	761	760	589
2007...........................	690	460	357	479	726	671	751	761	763	600
2008...........................	690	455	348	482	725	674	738	765	769	609
2009...........................	713	460	351	483	746	688	770	773	789	654
2010...........................	715	451	359	469	752	692	781	780	786	642
2011...........................	708	436	340	453	743	685	760	770	775	687
2012...........................	701	422	335	435	737	675	758	757	777	676
2013...........................	706	423	350	442	740	665	767	761	779	691
Men										
1979...........................	$874	$587	$464	$632	$940	$883	$1,006	$1,012	$934	$656
1980...........................	841	559	435	602	911	844	987	987	927	616
1981...........................	835	536	413	582	914	835	975	973	926	654
1982...........................	845	522	394	566	912	831	979	972	926	696
1983...........................	842	496	373	538	904	824	982	987	924	684
1984...........................	838	494	372	534	902	816	1,006	1,004	938	701
1985...........................	841	498	378	533	915	814	1,006	1,010	965	758
1986...........................	850	499	377	535	939	815	1,012	1,026	982	726
1987...........................	851	504	384	539	935	808	1,000	1,020	971	745
1988...........................	849	495	388	527	921	796	977	1,038	962	747
1989...........................	849	492	379	526	907	788	984	1,033	946	713
1990...........................	831	487	377	515	884	775	967	1,021	943	696
1991...........................	822	475	365	500	872	763	960	1,020	938	778
1992...........................	815	462	354	483	872	758	945	1,031	941	685
1993...........................	810	457	351	481	881	756	946	1,037	930	716
1994...........................	812	457	355	477	896	745	960	1,044	938	686
1995...........................	816	460	370	478	892	744	947	1,039	945	669
1996...........................	824	454	371	475	886	738	935	1,033	951	706
1997...........................	838	459	379	489	890	745	942	1,032	968	654
1998...........................	853	476	401	509	912	776	966	1,044	997	688
1999...........................	864	498	407	530	934	807	982	1,067	1,014	657
2000...........................	867	507	414	535	938	809	985	1,043	995	706
2001...........................	882	514	420	537	947	812	992	1,051	1,000	743
2002...........................	880	506	404	531	948	812	983	1,045	1,039	755
2003...........................	880	504	406	522	942	795	981	1,056	1,047	775
2004...........................	879	493	392	514	940	788	991	1,057	1,039	790
2005...........................	862	488	394	504	920	768	981	1,018	1,020	768
2006...........................	858	483	402	502	920	763	965	1,036	1,042	760
2007...........................	861	498	401	530	925	772	981	1,021	1,048	771
2008...........................	864	499	399	521	927	762	990	1,022	1,021	815
2009...........................	889	497	387	520	948	776	995	1,050	1,048	859
2010...........................	880	473	379	500	934	763	978	1,019	1,046	848
2011...........................	861	471	383	487	917	742	968	1,013	1,032	850
2012...........................	866	475	378	489	923	748	971	1,008	1,019	872
2013...........................	860	479	390	492	912	744	956	994	1,011	937

Note: The comparability of historical labor force data has been affected at various times by methodological and other changes in the Current

Population Survey (CPS). Information about historical comparability is online at www.bls.gov/cps/documentation.htm#comp. The Consumer Price Index research series using current methods (CPI-U-RS) is used to convert current dollars to constant (inflation-adjusted) dollars. See the technical notes section.

Source: U.S. Bureau of Labor Statistics.

Table 18. Inflation-adjusted median usual weekly earnings, by race and Hispanic or Latino ethnicity, for full-time wage and salary workers, 1979-2013 annual averages
[In constant 2013 dollars]

Year	Total, 16 years and older	White	Black or African American	Asian	Hispanic or Latino ethnicity
Total					
1979.	$722	$743	$596	–	$581
1980.	704	723	570	–	562
1981.	698	715	577	–	548
1982.	701	719	568	–	557
1983.	696	711	580	–	556
1984.	697	718	575	–	553
1985.	711	736	572	–	558
1986.	728	753	590	–	562
1987.	733	753	590	–	559
1988.	728	747	594	–	548
1989.	724	742	579	–	541
1990.	712	732	568	–	525
1991.	710	737	580	–	520
1992.	715	745	580	–	522
1993.	729	754	586	–	525
1994.	726	753	577	–	504
1995.	727	750	581	–	499
1996.	725	749	572	–	501
1997.	728	751	579	–	508
1998.	746	777	608	–	528
1999.	768	801	622	–	538
2000.	779	798	641	$832	540
2001.	784	803	646	841	549
2002.	788	807	645	852	549
2003.	785	805	651	877	557
2004.	787	810	647	873	562
2005.	777	802	621	899	562
2006.	775	797	640	905	561
2007.	781	804	639	933	565
2008.	781	803	637	932	573
2009.	802	822	653	955	587
2010.	798	817	653	913	572
2011.	783	802	637	896	568
2012.	779	803	630	933	576
2013.	776	802	629	942	578
Women					
1979.	$545	$551	$506	–	$470
1980.	540	546	497	–	462
1981.	538	543	506	–	467
1982.	555	561	503	–	471
1983.	560	564	516	–	478
1984.	566	573	515	–	476
1985.	572	581	521	–	475
1986.	590	596	535	–	489
1987.	594	602	541	–	492
1988.	595	601	544	–	491
1989.	595	606	546	–	488
1990.	598	610	532	–	480
1991.	610	622	538	–	487
1992.	618	629	545	–	491
1993.	624	637	552	–	497
1994.	621	635	538	–	474
1995.	616	630	539	–	463
1996.	618	633	536	–	467

Table 18. Inflation-adjusted median usual weekly earnings, by race and Hispanic or Latino ethnicity, for full-time wage and salary workers, 1979-2013 annual averages — Continued
[In constant 2013 dollars]

Year	Total, 16 years and older	White	Black or African American	Asian	Hispanic or Latino ethnicity
1997	624	643	543	–	460
1998	650	668	571	–	481
1999	662	676	572	–	487
2000	667	679	581	$740	495
2001	674	687	597	741	511
2002	685	709	613	733	514
2003	699	718	622	757	519
2004	707	720	623	756	517
2005	698	711	595	794	512
2006	693	703	599	807	508
2007	690	703	599	821	531
2008	690	708	600	815	542
2009	713	726	632	846	553
2010	715	731	632	826	543
2011	708	728	616	777	536
2012	701	720	608	781	528
2013	706	722	606	819	541
Men					
1979	$874	$892	$680	–	$656
1980	841	860	656	–	629
1981	835	860	658	–	617
1982	845	870	645	–	624
1983	842	860	653	–	609
1984	838	857	647	–	613
1985	841	864	630	–	612
1986	850	878	647	–	606
1987	851	882	641	–	600
1988	849	879	658	–	582
1989	849	875	632	–	572
1990	831	853	623	–	549
1991	822	843	625	–	538
1992	815	836	618	–	551
1993	810	832	622	–	549
1994	812	851	622	–	533
1995	816	859	624	–	531
1996	824	858	609	–	527
1997	838	861	625	–	537
1998	853	877	668	–	556
1999	864	892	683	–	568
2000	867	896	690	$927	564
2001	882	907	696	963	579
2002	880	909	679	979	584
2003	880	905	703	977	587
2004	879	903	702	989	592
2005	862	887	667	984	584
2006	858	879	682	1,018	583
2007	861	885	674	1,052	584
2008	864	893	671	1,045	605
2009	889	917	674	1,034	618
2010	880	908	676	1,000	598
2011	861	886	676	1,004	591
2012	866	891	674	1,070	600
2013	860	884	664	1,059	594

Note: The comparability of historical labor force data has been affected at various times by methodological and other changes in the Current Population Survey (CPS). Information about historical comparability is online at www.bls.gov/cps/documentation.htm#comp. As of 2003, estimates for the race groups shown (White, Black or African American, and Asian) include people who selected that race group only; people who selected more than one race group are not included. Prior to 2003, people who reported more than one race were included in the group they identified as the main

race. Asian data for 2000-2002 are for Asians and Pacific Islanders. As of 2003, Asians constitute a separate category. Data for Asians were not tabulated prior to 2000. People of Hispanic or Latino ethnicity may be of any race; estimates for the race groups include Hispanics. The Consumer Price Index research series using current methods (CPI-U-RS) is used to convert current dollars to constant (inflation-adjusted) dollars. See the technical notes section. Dash indicates data not available.
Source: U.S. Bureau of Labor Statistics.

Table 19. Inflation-adjusted median usual weekly earnings, by educational attainment, for full-time wage and salary workers 25 years and older, 1979-2013 annual averages
[In constant 2013 dollars]

Year	Total, 25 years and older	Less than a high school diploma	High school graduates, no college	Some college or associate degree	Bachelor's degree and higher
Total					
1979	$793	$629	$746	$844	$1,030
1980	769	597	715	817	1,011
1981	757	590	703	796	1,000
1982	759	575	701	814	1,016
1983	762	569	691	807	1,024
1984	774	562	690	816	1,038
1985	783	558	688	824	1,045
1986	793	564	698	830	1,065
1987	790	557	698	825	1,106
1988	783	544	696	813	1,106
1989	775	539	681	820	1,105
1990	775	523	667	822	1,102
1991	778	512	662	815	1,110
1992	779	506	655	787	1,132
1993	779	498	659	784	1,135
1994	778	477	655	776	1,140
1995	774	469	656	771	1,134
1996	769	469	655	766	1,121
1997	781	465	667	774	1,127
1998	816	481	683	796	1,171
1999	828	484	685	811	1,203
2000	824	490	683	806	1,206
2001	829	503	684	812	1,212
2002	837	503	693	815	1,219
2003	838	501	701	809	1,220
2004	842	494	708	815	1,216
2005	831	488	696	800	1,209
2006	829	484	687	799	1,200
2007	829	481	679	791	1,204
2008	824	490	669	781	1,207
2009	840	493	680	788	1,235
2010	835	474	669	784	1,222
2011	825	467	660	765	1,190
2012	827	478	661	760	1,182
2013	827	472	651	748	1,194
Women					
1979	$584	$455	$554	$632	$790
1980	573	441	540	621	780
1981	572	430	533	627	781
1982	592	427	548	636	803
1983	596	433	547	640	820
1984	605	427	553	652	833
1985	612	417	554	655	855
1986	625	422	562	669	884
1987	629	420	565	680	914
1988	633	418	563	681	917
1989	637	419	552	688	920
1990	637	415	544	682	924
1991	645	417	547	682	937
1992	650	416	548	662	966
1993	659	417	551	670	970
1994	655	400	546	658	986
1995	649	398	540	648	977
1996	657	396	540	654	972

Table 19. Inflation-adjusted median usual weekly earnings, by educational attainment, for full-time wage and salary workers 25 years and older, 1979-2013 annual averages — Continued
[In constant 2013 dollars]

Year	Total, 25 years and older	Less than a high school diploma	High school graduates, no college	Some college or associate degree	Bachelor's degree and higher
1997	669	398	547	664	973
1998	692	404	565	679	1,009
1999	695	406	566	683	1,035
2000	698	411	568	683	1,023
2001	714	416	583	684	1,034
2002	736	421	593	703	1,048
2003	739	416	600	709	1,053
2004	739	412	602	711	1,060
2005	730	407	588	700	1,054
2006	724	413	577	695	1,045
2007	726	415	575	684	1,047
2008	725	409	563	680	1,034
2009	746	415	588	684	1,053
2010	752	415	580	682	1,053
2011	743	409	573	668	1,033
2012	737	391	569	668	1,015
2013	740	400	573	657	1,043
Men					
1979	$940	$754	$922	$985	$1,186
1980	911	718	879	962	1,148
1981	914	703	875	956	1,167
1982	912	680	868	954	1,167
1983	904	669	862	938	1,151
1984	902	658	853	953	1,201
1985	915	649	841	975	1,219
1986	939	651	844	984	1,254
1987	935	635	829	975	1,280
1988	921	628	826	951	1,284
1989	907	628	817	938	1,279
1990	884	603	793	936	1,280
1991	872	582	783	938	1,273
1992	872	571	779	902	1,286
1993	881	565	773	908	1,279
1994	896	532	771	913	1,285
1995	892	527	769	904	1,282
1996	886	528	763	893	1,293
1997	890	528	774	899	1,297
1998	912	546	797	917	1,340
1999	934	552	811	930	1,366
2000	938	549	800	935	1,380
2001	947	551	801	951	1,404
2002	948	545	799	947	1,412
2003	942	543	795	937	1,432
2004	940	550	795	938	1,409
2005	920	543	778	914	1,393
2006	920	542	783	919	1,391
2007	925	540	774	910	1,397
2008	927	538	767	898	1,391
2009	948	543	777	907	1,441
2010	934	519	759	903	1,421
2011	917	505	745	870	1,379
2012	923	515	745	869	1,390
2013	912	500	732	858	1,395

Note: The comparability of historical labor force data has been affected at various times by methodological and other changes in the Current Population Survey (CPS). Information about historical comparability is online at www.bls.gov/cps/documentation.htm#comp. The Consumer Price Index research series using current methods (CPI-U-RS) is used to convert current dollars to constant (inflation-adjusted) dollars. See the technical

notes section.
Source: U.S. Bureau of Labor Statistics.

Table 20. Inflation-adjusted median hourly earnings, by age, for wage and salary workers paid hourly rates, 1979-2013 annual averages
[In constant 2013 dollars]

Year	Total, 16 years and older	16 to 24 years			25 years and older					
		Total	16 to 19 years	20 to 24 years	Total	25 to 34 years	35 to 44 years	45 to 54 years	55 to 64 years	65 years and older
Total										
1979...	$13.29	$10.45	$9.28	$12.04	$15.30	$15.57	$15.84	$15.45	$14.88	$9.67
1980...	12.96	9.97	8.66	11.53	14.92	15.22	15.48	15.19	14.49	9.57
1981...	12.65	9.75	8.80	11.33	14.72	14.96	15.23	14.77	14.28	9.63
1982...	12.53	9.40	8.35	10.81	14.57	14.73	15.34	14.90	14.18	9.56
1983...	12.42	9.07	8.02	10.42	14.56	14.44	15.36	14.96	14.24	9.78
1984...	12.46	8.93	7.80	10.30	14.62	14.47	15.32	15.13	14.15	9.89
1985...	12.46	8.80	7.58	10.21	14.57	14.30	15.48	15.23	14.28	9.79
1986...	12.58	8.95	7.53	10.26	14.67	14.22	15.80	15.68	14.54	10.08
1987...	12.69	9.00	7.47	10.22	14.63	14.10	15.57	15.41	14.55	9.96
1988...	12.72	9.05	7.62	10.17	14.63	14.05	15.44	15.43	14.14	9.89
1989...	12.69	8.98	7.66	10.25	14.41	13.87	15.54	15.28	14.19	9.84
1990...	12.49	8.91	7.75	10.21	14.09	13.64	15.23	15.18	13.85	9.93
1991...	12.50	8.77	7.82	10.00	14.13	13.40	15.28	15.18	13.65	9.90
1992...	12.55	8.73	7.69	9.80	14.20	13.28	15.25	15.48	13.79	9.98
1993...	12.49	8.75	7.62	9.76	14.21	13.13	15.25	15.65	14.13	10.14
1994...	12.46	8.74	7.64	9.67	14.18	13.03	15.43	15.58	14.03	9.94
1995...	12.40	8.80	7.65	9.74	14.20	13.22	15.20	15.37	13.96	10.09
1996...	12.43	8.79	7.65	9.90	14.23	13.05	15.00	15.15	13.89	10.01
1997...	12.66	8.90	7.97	10.00	14.28	13.08	14.99	15.34	14.08	9.97
1998...	12.98	9.39	8.39	10.33	14.45	13.77	15.49	15.63	14.38	10.56
1999...	13.33	9.61	8.50	10.83	14.64	13.96	15.41	15.85	14.52	10.77
2000...	13.41	9.80	8.67	10.92	14.72	13.78	15.36	15.99	14.64	10.89
2001...	13.41	10.12	8.89	11.03	15.00	14.04	15.75	16.01	14.96	11.22
2002...	13.56	10.12	8.95	10.97	15.32	14.22	15.78	16.14	15.35	11.75
2003...	13.73	10.00	8.77	10.96	15.25	14.24	15.77	16.42	15.43	11.63
2004...	13.56	9.84	8.63	10.83	15.08	14.02	15.89	16.31	15.51	11.86
2005...	13.35	9.63	8.41	10.63	14.89	14.03	15.64	16.09	15.45	11.85
2006...	13.58	9.52	8.35	10.58	14.94	13.80	15.58	16.20	15.39	11.72
2007...	13.43	9.72	8.51	10.85	14.79	13.54	15.65	16.17	15.40	11.65
2008...	13.24	9.60	8.48	10.56	14.95	13.53	15.56	16.09	15.37	11.79
2009...	13.51	9.66	8.60	10.61	15.10	13.68	15.84	16.12	15.96	12.48
2010...	13.35	9.51	8.55	10.18	14.94	13.39	15.61	16.00	15.91	12.34
2011...	13.16	9.29	8.34	9.95	14.62	13.16	15.35	15.53	15.60	12.62
2012...	12.98	9.18	8.22	9.84	14.45	13.00	15.07	15.28	15.61	12.38
2013...	12.93	9.16	8.19	9.83	14.50	12.88	14.98	15.17	15.62	12.47
Women										
1979...	$10.84	$9.55	$9.07	$10.54	$11.68	$12.10	$11.89	$11.50	$11.23	$9.34
1980...	10.62	9.27	8.44	10.19	11.40	11.94	11.53	11.37	10.97	9.09
1981...	10.52	9.12	8.65	10.05	11.52	12.01	11.72	11.28	10.88	9.12
1982...	10.70	8.77	8.24	9.72	11.65	12.04	11.79	11.48	11.14	9.12
1983...	10.67	8.49	7.89	9.47	11.62	12.09	11.80	11.53	11.27	9.24
1984...	10.62	8.40	7.67	9.32	11.71	11.97	11.99	11.77	11.26	9.34
1985...	10.60	8.29	7.46	9.42	11.84	11.96	12.21	11.90	11.28	9.15
1986...	10.81	8.34	7.40	9.55	12.07	12.07	12.43	12.15	11.66	9.59
1987...	10.98	8.27	7.27	9.59	12.08	12.04	12.45	12.31	11.82	9.51
1988...	11.04	8.47	7.39	9.55	12.17	12.02	12.78	12.46	11.49	9.68
1989...	11.09	8.51	7.44	9.49	12.30	12.12	12.89	12.52	11.58	9.33
1990...	11.12	8.55	7.51	9.62	12.21	12.11	12.73	12.37	11.62	9.41
1991...	11.25	8.47	7.73	9.52	12.23	11.98	12.88	12.68	11.58	9.60
1992...	11.32	8.39	7.63	9.38	12.44	12.11	12.99	12.91	11.71	9.71
1993...	11.30	8.37	7.51	9.46	12.49	12.08	12.95	12.98	12.00	9.81
1994...	11.28	8.27	7.51	9.30	12.52	12.10	13.13	13.16	12.16	9.70
1995...	11.32	8.33	7.50	9.24	12.40	12.02	13.10	13.23	12.03	9.79

Table 20. Inflation-adjusted median hourly earnings, by age, for wage and salary workers paid hourly rates, 1979-2013 annual averages — Continued
[In constant 2013 dollars]

Year	Total, 16 years and older	16 to 24 years			25 years and older					
		Total	16 to 19 years	20 to 24 years	Total	25 to 34 years	35 to 44 years	45 to 54 years	55 to 64 years	65 years and older
1996	11.43	8.40	7.53	9.26	12.47	11.92	13.15	13.22	11.94	9.54
1997	11.49	8.61	7.84	9.48	12.66	11.87	13.23	13.40	12.03	9.88
1998	11.74	8.90	8.25	9.89	13.02	12.55	13.78	13.95	12.62	10.29
1999	12.08	9.23	8.36	10.10	13.33	12.73	13.75	13.92	13.05	10.49
2000	12.26	9.47	8.43	10.55	13.38	13.11	13.57	13.78	13.32	10.65
2001	12.68	9.54	8.70	10.53	13.42	13.08	13.74	14.28	13.67	10.71
2002	12.81	9.65	8.81	10.51	13.87	13.11	14.22	14.48	14.00	11.31
2003	12.76	9.61	8.67	10.37	13.94	13.30	14.14	14.92	13.99	11.19
2004	12.54	9.51	8.46	10.26	13.85	13.09	14.12	14.73	14.27	11.29
2005	12.30	9.31	8.26	10.14	13.82	12.96	14.13	14.47	14.15	11.72
2006	12.30	9.23	8.21	10.18	13.71	12.78	13.91	14.16	14.00	11.51
2007	12.34	9.16	8.33	10.11	13.54	12.60	13.89	14.44	13.74	11.40
2008	12.44	9.12	8.34	9.91	13.51	12.68	13.95	14.24	14.07	11.40
2009	12.77	9.32	8.49	9.98	13.85	12.99	14.12	14.21	14.76	12.06
2010	12.64	9.21	8.45	9.70	13.76	12.86	14.02	14.42	14.62	11.94
2011	12.40	9.04	8.24	9.48	13.56	12.55	13.91	14.24	14.52	12.17
2012	12.16	8.90	8.13	9.30	13.36	12.32	13.65	14.00	14.56	12.01
2013	12.12	8.93	8.09	9.40	13.36	12.23	13.77	13.94	14.53	12.22
Men										
1979	$16.92	$11.68	$9.55	$13.89	$20.03	$19.10	$21.32	$21.26	$19.73	$10.66
1980	16.40	11.02	9.06	13.23	19.41	18.63	20.99	20.91	19.46	10.19
1981	16.14	10.59	8.94	12.56	19.12	18.01	20.39	20.86	19.36	10.34
1982	15.89	10.16	8.49	11.88	18.75	17.80	20.63	20.60	18.89	10.35
1983	15.38	9.73	8.16	11.22	18.47	17.20	20.49	20.36	19.42	10.56
1984	15.21	9.76	7.95	11.03	18.38	16.84	20.32	20.71	18.93	10.49
1985	15.14	9.67	7.75	10.81	18.29	16.53	20.25	20.60	18.68	10.31
1986	15.40	9.72	7.75	11.01	18.30	16.29	20.26	20.59	19.35	10.51
1987	15.24	9.63	7.75	11.14	17.96	16.20	19.80	20.08	19.06	10.43
1988	14.95	9.51	7.83	10.95	17.73	15.90	19.32	20.21	18.41	10.43
1989	14.70	9.38	7.97	10.93	17.62	15.54	19.22	19.75	18.15	10.71
1990	14.28	9.40	8.01	10.67	16.99	15.25	18.53	19.22	17.56	10.50
1991	14.32	9.30	7.90	10.38	16.63	14.90	18.30	19.52	16.80	10.37
1992	14.10	9.19	7.80	10.15	16.36	14.67	17.77	19.54	16.89	10.49
1993	14.06	9.13	7.73	10.05	16.16	14.44	17.71	19.29	17.40	10.65
1994	14.00	9.14	7.74	10.20	16.00	14.15	17.88	18.82	17.20	10.33
1995	14.01	9.17	7.80	10.35	16.28	14.36	18.04	18.69	16.86	10.39
1996	14.08	9.13	7.77	10.34	15.95	14.35	17.62	18.34	16.49	10.41
1997	14.23	9.33	8.12	10.39	16.06	14.36	17.47	18.52	17.06	10.07
1998	14.35	9.86	8.53	11.10	16.72	14.58	17.80	18.60	17.43	11.04
1999	14.42	9.96	8.64	11.23	16.78	15.16	17.87	19.13	17.08	10.99
2000	14.63	10.32	8.99	11.35	16.56	14.84	17.78	18.81	17.33	11.24
2001	14.89	10.54	9.08	11.74	16.95	15.24	18.32	18.75	17.04	11.84
2002	15.08	10.43	9.09	11.50	16.90	15.40	18.08	18.65	17.33	12.67
2003	15.05	10.30	8.89	11.39	16.77	15.20	17.89	18.90	17.84	12.39
2004	14.82	10.12	8.82	11.18	16.94	14.83	18.00	18.63	17.93	12.21
2005	14.51	10.05	8.60	10.98	16.60	14.52	17.76	18.05	17.65	11.98
2006	14.64	10.15	8.58	11.26	16.48	14.58	17.39	18.52	17.37	12.38
2007	14.55	10.26	8.73	11.19	16.57	14.42	17.04	18.15	17.36	12.37
2008	14.57	10.00	8.64	10.82	16.27	14.58	17.34	18.20	17.21	12.45
2009	14.94	10.01	8.74	10.85	16.36	14.33	17.48	18.45	17.47	13.03
2010	14.70	9.84	8.64	10.58	16.07	14.00	16.91	18.04	17.57	12.74
2011	14.29	9.55	8.45	10.25	15.64	13.64	16.59	17.47	17.67	13.30
2012	14.08	9.57	8.31	10.11	15.39	13.47	16.28	17.23	17.53	13.22
2013	14.00	9.67	8.37	10.00	15.27	13.42	16.21	17.17	17.28	12.88

Note: The comparability of historical labor force data has been affected at various times by methodological and other changes in the Current

Population Survey (CPS). Information about historical comparability is online at www.bls.gov/cps/documentation.htm#comp. The Consumer Price Index research series using current methods (CPI-U-RS) is used to convert current dollars to constant (inflation-adjusted) dollars. See the technical notes section.
Source: U.S. Bureau of Labor Statistics.

Table 21. Inflation-adjusted median hourly earnings, by race and Hispanic or Latino ethnicity, for wage and salary workers paid hourly rates, 1979-2013 annual averages
[In constant 2013 dollars]

Year	Total, 16 years and older	White	Black or African American	Asian	Hispanic or Latino ethnicity
Total					
1979	$13.29	$13.50	$12.31	–	$12.22
1980	12.96	13.12	11.94	–	11.94
1981	12.65	12.73	12.04	–	11.82
1982	12.53	12.69	11.74	–	11.62
1983	12.42	12.58	11.44	–	11.31
1984	12.46	12.61	11.45	–	11.26
1985	12.46	12.60	11.36	–	11.30
1986	12.58	12.74	11.76	–	11.46
1987	12.69	12.86	11.75	–	11.41
1988	12.72	12.87	11.63	–	11.25
1989	12.69	12.85	11.67	–	11.02
1990	12.49	12.66	11.76	–	10.85
1991	12.50	12.68	11.67	–	10.77
1992	12.55	12.72	11.48	–	10.81
1993	12.49	12.65	11.40	–	10.84
1994	12.46	12.61	11.34	–	10.78
1995	12.40	12.63	11.62	–	10.62
1996	12.43	12.68	11.48	–	10.61
1997	12.66	12.85	11.59	–	10.69
1998	12.98	13.15	11.97	–	11.30
1999	13.33	13.62	12.38	–	11.29
2000	13.41	13.48	12.64	$13.63	11.56
2001	13.41	13.50	12.87	14.14	11.92
2002	13.56	13.87	12.86	13.42	11.94
2003	13.73	13.89	12.85	14.08	12.35
2004	13.56	13.72	12.56	13.69	12.10
2005	13.35	13.70	12.14	14.33	11.87
2006	13.58	13.70	12.31	14.47	11.69
2007	13.43	13.57	12.24	13.73	11.51
2008	13.24	13.57	12.12	14.08	11.87
2009	13.51	13.75	12.64	14.29	11.99
2010	13.35	13.61	12.57	14.12	11.62
2011	13.16	13.36	12.20	13.82	11.44
2012	12.98	13.23	12.01	13.42	11.28
2013	12.93	13.15	11.90	13.62	11.25
Women					
1979	$10.84	$10.84	$10.63	–	$10.30
1980	10.62	10.65	10.43	–	10.16
1981	10.52	10.52	10.29	–	10.07
1982	10.70	10.70	10.42	–	10.05
1983	10.67	10.69	10.49	–	9.82
1984	10.62	10.64	10.41	–	9.94
1985	10.60	10.62	10.41	–	9.96
1986	10.81	10.85	10.49	–	10.14
1987	10.98	11.02	10.59	–	10.02
1988	11.04	11.08	10.60	–	9.98
1989	11.09	11.13	10.67	–	10.04
1990	11.12	11.16	10.76	–	10.02
1991	11.25	11.27	10.92	–	9.97
1992	11.32	11.37	10.80	–	10.03
1993	11.30	11.37	10.90	–	10.02
1994	11.28	11.42	10.78	–	9.95
1995	11.32	11.44	10.80	–	10.02

Table 21. Inflation-adjusted median hourly earnings, by race and Hispanic or Latino ethnicity, for wage and salary workers paid hourly rates, 1979-2013 annual averages — Continued
[In constant 2013 dollars]

Year	Total, 16 years and older	White	Black or African American	Asian	Hispanic or Latino ethnicity
1996	11.43	11.52	10.65	–	10.01
1997	11.49	11.58	10.98	–	9.87
1998	11.74	11.88	11.27	–	10.30
1999	12.08	12.21	11.37	–	10.43
2000	12.26	12.30	11.99	$13.22	10.68
2001	12.68	12.80	12.04	13.25	10.89
2002	12.81	12.88	12.24	13.08	11.06
2003	12.76	12.80	12.54	13.52	11.24
2004	12.54	12.59	12.24	13.03	11.15
2005	12.30	12.53	11.85	13.89	10.95
2006	12.30	12.44	11.67	13.80	10.97
2007	12.34	12.43	11.74	13.29	11.01
2008	12.44	12.66	11.67	13.26	10.90
2009	12.77	12.84	11.95	13.76	10.96
2010	12.64	12.69	11.97	13.26	10.80
2011	12.40	12.47	11.68	13.25	10.61
2012	12.16	12.25	11.39	12.93	10.35
2013	12.12	12.21	11.54	13.04	10.49
Men					
1979	$16.92	$17.34	$14.64	–	$14.34
1980	16.40	16.75	13.92	–	13.52
1981	16.14	16.49	14.28	–	13.19
1982	15.89	16.19	13.85	–	13.29
1983	15.38	15.71	13.24	–	12.91
1984	15.21	15.51	13.16	–	12.91
1985	15.14	15.66	12.71	–	12.54
1986	15.40	15.78	13.33	–	12.56
1987	15.24	15.55	13.22	–	12.49
1988	14.95	15.24	13.12	–	12.31
1989	14.70	15.03	12.83	–	12.09
1990	14.28	14.77	12.73	–	11.64
1991	14.32	14.70	12.62	–	11.47
1992	14.10	14.46	12.39	–	11.37
1993	14.06	14.40	12.17	–	11.30
1994	14.00	14.32	12.32	–	11.15
1995	14.01	14.60	12.38	–	11.02
1996	14.08	14.48	12.10	–	11.27
1997	14.23	14.41	12.55	–	11.43
1998	14.35	14.52	12.97	–	11.75
1999	14.42	14.84	13.66	–	12.04
2000	14.63	14.82	13.50	$14.60	12.23
2001	14.89	15.28	13.39	15.58	12.72
2002	15.08	15.36	13.26	14.27	12.85
2003	15.05	15.23	13.68	15.05	12.70
2004	14.82	14.99	13.42	14.67	12.36
2005	14.51	14.88	13.01	15.21	12.16
2006	14.64	14.87	13.19	15.22	12.52
2007	14.55	14.85	13.00	14.85	12.44
2008	14.57	14.99	12.98	15.18	12.80
2009	14.94	15.15	13.32	15.21	12.94
2010	14.70	14.93	12.99	15.07	12.53
2011	14.29	14.51	12.48	14.75	12.23
2012	14.08	14.37	12.37	14.35	12.13
2013	14.00	14.24	12.16	14.24	11.99

Note: The comparability of historical labor force data has been affected at various times by methodological and other changes in the Current

Population Survey (CPS). Information about historical comparability is online at www.bls.gov/cps/documentation.htm#comp. As of 2003, estimates for the race groups shown (White, Black or African American, and Asian) include people who selected that race group only; people who selected more than one race group are not included. Prior to 2003, people who reported more than one race were included in the group they identified as the main race. Asian data for 2000-2002 are for Asians and Pacific Islanders. As of 2003, Asians constitute a separate category. Data for Asians were not tabulated prior to 2000. People of Hispanic or Latino ethnicity may be of any race; estimates for the race groups include Hispanics. The Consumer Price Index research series using current methods (CPI-U-RS) is used to convert current dollars to constant (inflation-adjusted) dollars. See the technical notes section. Dash indicates data not available.
Source: U.S. Bureau of Labor Statistics.

Table 22. Median usual weekly earnings of full-time wage and salary workers, by age, 1979-2013 annual averages
[In current dollars]

Year	Total, 16 years and older	16 to 24 years			25 years and older					
		Total	16 to 19 years	20 to 24 years	Total	25 to 34 years	35 to 44 years	45 to 54 years	55 to 64 years	65 years and older
Total										
1979...	$241	$172	$144	$186	$265	$255	$280	$276	$262	$198
1980...	262	187	154	200	286	276	302	298	285	203
1981...	284	200	161	213	308	296	326	320	309	222
1982...	302	208	164	220	327	311	354	345	325	253
1983...	313	211	164	223	343	321	370	367	346	261
1984...	326	217	169	231	362	335	389	385	366	272
1985...	344	224	174	240	379	349	406	400	381	297
1986...	359	232	178	248	391	360	419	416	397	298
1987...	374	243	186	259	403	373	435	429	405	310
1988...	385	249	196	266	414	383	450	453	419	323
1989...	399	259	204	276	427	394	472	472	431	334
1990...	412	269	209	285	449	407	486	489	457	343
1991...	426	277	213	291	467	415	498	507	469	381
1992...	440	276	212	290	479	422	503	522	483	378
1993...	459	282	214	297	491	436	517	542	492	393
1994...	467	286	221	300	500	439	537	566	501	384
1995...	479	292	231	306	510	451	550	582	514	389
1996...	490	298	240	312	520	463	559	594	535	384
1997...	503	306	252	321	540	481	579	607	558	393
1998...	523	319	268	339	572	502	597	620	592	405
1999...	549	341	281	363	592	518	611	652	604	404
2000...	576	361	297	383	609	549	625	669	620	463
2001...	596	375	305	394	630	576	657	693	638	488
2002...	608	381	305	399	646	591	668	706	674	502
2003...	620	387	311	402	662	594	687	723	708	516
2004...	638	390	309	406	683	604	713	743	725	560
2005...	651	397	318	411	696	610	731	748	742	569
2006...	671	409	324	423	718	621	748	773	765	583
2007...	695	424	337	450	738	643	769	790	803	605
2008...	722	443	349	467	761	666	804	822	825	644
2009...	739	442	344	464	774	678	817	838	841	684
2010...	747	432	347	454	782	682	824	844	860	684
2011...	756	440	352	457	797	693	837	866	881	742
2012...	768	444	356	464	815	707	858	878	897	757
2013...	776	454	373	472	827	708	874	883	904	801
Women										
1979...	$182	$154	$132	$161	$195	$199	$196	$192	$189	$170
1980...	201	167	145	175	213	218	214	209	205	175
1981...	219	180	154	191	233	239	238	225	222	189
1982...	239	192	158	201	255	258	258	252	245	211
1983...	252	198	158	207	268	272	272	264	257	212
1984...	265	203	162	213	283	285	292	279	270	219
1985...	277	211	166	221	296	296	307	292	285	242
1986...	291	219	170	231	308	306	319	308	296	256
1987...	303	227	172	242	321	316	337	324	308	261
1988...	315	235	184	251	335	327	354	339	317	280
1989...	328	246	197	260	351	340	370	357	333	292
1990...	346	254	198	269	369	356	390	377	348	300
1991...	366	266	205	280	387	371	407	398	363	319
1992...	380	267	205	280	400	382	418	417	376	328
1993...	393	273	205	289	415	395	435	440	395	335
1994...	399	276	211	290	421	397	448	450	398	336
1995...	406	275	215	291	428	403	453	464	403	353

Table 22. Median usual weekly earnings of full-time wage and salary workers, by age, 1979-2013 annual averages — Continued

[In current dollars]

Year	Total, 16 years and older	16 to 24 years			25 years and older					
		Total	16 to 19 years	20 to 24 years	Total	25 to 34 years	35 to 44 years	45 to 54 years	55 to 64 years	65 years and older
1996............	418	284	223	298	444	415	463	481	420	334
1997............	431	292	240	306	462	427	482	495	433	348
1998............	456	305	249	319	485	451	498	516	476	350
1999............	473	324	266	343	497	470	503	534	492	370
2000............	493	344	283	366	516	493	521	564	508	392
2001............	512	353	288	375	543	512	547	587	536	390
2002............	529	367	295	385	568	530	571	602	574	430
2003............	552	371	299	387	584	546	590	609	601	435
2004............	573	375	293	391	599	561	608	625	615	478
2005............	585	381	304	396	612	573	621	644	639	492
2006............	600	395	305	413	627	583	645	659	658	510
2007............	614	409	318	426	646	597	668	677	679	534
2008............	638	420	322	445	670	623	682	707	711	563
2009............	657	424	323	445	687	634	709	712	727	602
2010............	669	422	336	439	704	648	731	730	736	601
2011............	684	421	328	438	718	662	734	744	749	664
2012............	691	416	330	429	727	666	747	746	766	667
2013............	706	423	350	442	740	665	767	761	779	691
Men										
1979............	$292	$196	$155	$211	$314	$295	$336	$338	$312	$219
1980............	313	208	162	224	339	314	367	367	345	229
1981............	340	218	168	237	372	340	397	396	377	266
1982............	364	225	170	244	393	358	422	419	399	300
1983............	379	223	168	242	407	371	442	444	416	308
1984............	392	231	174	250	422	382	471	470	439	328
1985............	407	241	183	258	443	394	487	489	467	367
1986............	419	246	186	264	463	402	499	506	484	358
1987............	434	257	196	275	477	412	510	520	495	380
1988............	449	262	205	279	487	421	517	549	509	395
1989............	468	271	209	290	500	434	542	569	521	393
1990............	481	282	218	298	512	449	560	591	546	403
1991............	493	285	219	300	523	458	576	612	563	467
1992............	501	284	218	297	536	466	581	634	579	421
1993............	510	288	221	303	555	476	596	653	586	451
1994............	522	294	228	307	576	479	617	671	603	441
1995............	538	303	244	315	588	490	624	685	623	441
1996............	557	307	251	321	599	499	632	698	643	477
1997............	579	317	262	338	615	515	651	713	669	452
1998............	598	334	281	357	639	544	677	732	699	482
1999............	618	356	291	379	668	577	702	763	725	470
2000............	641	375	306	395	693	598	728	771	735	522
2001............	670	391	319	408	720	617	754	799	760	565
2002............	679	391	312	410	732	627	759	807	802	583
2003............	695	398	321	412	744	628	775	834	827	612
2004............	713	400	318	417	762	639	804	857	843	641
2005............	722	409	330	422	771	644	822	853	855	644
2006............	743	418	348	435	797	661	836	897	902	658
2007............	766	443	357	472	823	687	873	909	933	686
2008............	798	461	369	481	857	704	915	944	943	753
2009............	819	458	356	479	873	715	916	967	965	791
2010............	824	443	355	468	874	714	915	954	979	794
2011............	832	455	370	470	886	717	935	979	997	821
2012............	854	468	373	482	910	738	957	994	1,005	860
2013............	860	479	390	492	912	744	956	994	1,011	937

Note: The comparability of historical labor force data has been affected at various times by methodological and other changes in the Current

Population Survey (CPS). Information about historical comparability is online at www.bls.gov/cps/documentation.htm#comp.
Source: U.S. Bureau of Labor Statistics.

Table 23. Median usual weekly earnings of full-time wage and salary workers, by race and Hispanic or Latino ethnicity, 1979-2013 annual averages
[In current dollars]

Year	Total, 16 years and older	White	Black or African American	Asian	Hispanic or Latino ethnicity
Total					
1979..	$241	$248	$199	–	$194
1980..	262	269	212	–	209
1981..	284	291	235	–	223
1982..	302	310	245	–	240
1983..	313	320	261	–	250
1984..	326	336	269	–	259
1985..	344	356	277	–	270
1986..	359	371	291	–	277
1987..	374	384	301	–	285
1988..	385	395	314	–	290
1989..	399	409	319	–	298
1990..	412	424	329	–	304
1991..	426	442	348	–	312
1992..	440	458	357	–	321
1993..	459	475	369	–	331
1994..	467	484	371	–	324
1995..	479	494	383	–	329
1996..	490	506	387	–	339
1997..	503	519	400	–	351
1998..	523	545	426	–	370
1999..	549	573	445	–	385
2000..	576	590	474	$615	399
2001..	596	610	491	639	417
2002..	608	623	498	658	424
2003..	620	636	514	693	440
2004..	638	657	525	708	456
2005..	651	672	520	753	471
2006..	671	690	554	784	486
2007..	695	716	569	830	503
2008..	722	742	589	861	529
2009..	739	757	601	880	541
2010..	747	765	611	855	535
2011..	756	775	615	866	549
2012..	768	792	621	920	568
2013..	776	802	629	942	578
Women					
1979..	$182	$184	$169	–	$157
1980..	201	203	185	–	172
1981..	219	221	206	–	190
1982..	239	242	217	–	203
1983..	252	254	232	–	215
1984..	265	268	241	–	223
1985..	277	281	252	–	230
1986..	291	294	264	–	241
1987..	303	307	276	–	251
1988..	315	318	288	–	260
1989..	328	334	301	–	269
1990..	346	353	308	–	278
1991..	366	373	323	–	292
1992..	380	387	335	–	302
1993..	393	401	348	–	313
1994..	399	408	346	–	305
1995..	406	415	355	–	305

Table 23. Median usual weekly earnings of full-time wage and salary workers, by race and Hispanic or Latino ethnicity, 1979-2013 annual averages — Continued
[In current dollars]

Year	Total, 16 years and older	White	Black or African American	Asian	Hispanic or Latino ethnicity
1996.	418	428	362	–	316
1997.	431	444	375	–	318
1998.	456	468	400	–	337
1999.	473	483	409	–	348
2000.	493	502	429	$547	366
2001.	512	522	454	563	388
2002.	529	547	473	566	397
2003.	552	567	491	598	410
2004.	573	584	505	613	419
2005.	585	596	499	665	429
2006.	600	609	519	699	440
2007.	614	626	533	731	473
2008.	638	654	554	753	501
2009.	657	669	582	779	509
2010.	669	684	592	773	508
2011.	684	703	595	751	518
2012.	691	710	599	770	521
2013.	706	722	606	819	541
Men					
1979.	$292	$298	$227	–	$219
1980.	313	320	244	–	234
1981.	340	350	268	–	251
1982.	364	375	278	–	269
1983.	379	387	294	–	274
1984.	392	401	303	–	287
1985.	407	418	305	–	296
1986.	419	433	319	–	299
1987.	434	450	327	–	306
1988.	449	465	348	–	308
1989.	468	482	348	–	315
1990.	481	494	361	–	318
1991.	493	506	375	–	323
1992.	501	514	380	–	339
1993.	510	524	392	–	346
1994.	522	547	400	–	343
1995.	538	566	411	–	350
1996.	557	580	412	–	356
1997.	579	595	432	–	371
1998.	598	615	468	–	390
1999.	618	638	488	–	406
2000.	641	662	510	$685	417
2001.	670	689	529	732	440
2002.	679	702	524	756	451
2003.	695	715	555	772	464
2004.	713	732	569	802	480
2005.	722	743	559	825	489
2006.	743	761	591	882	505
2007.	766	788	600	936	520
2008.	798	825	620	966	559
2009.	819	845	621	952	569
2010.	824	850	633	936	560
2011.	832	856	653	970	571
2012.	854	879	665	1,055	592
2013.	860	884	664	1,059	594

Note: The comparability of historical labor force data has been affected at various times by methodological and other changes in the Current

Population Survey (CPS). Information about historical comparability is online at www.bls.gov/cps/documentation.htm#comp. As of 2003, estimates for the race groups shown (White, Black or African American, and Asian) include people who selected that race group only; people who selected more than one race group are not included. Prior to 2003, people who reported more than one race were included in the group they identified as the main race. Asian data for 2000-2002 are for Asians and Pacific Islanders. As of 2003, Asians constitute a separate category. Data for Asians were not tabulated prior to 2000. People of Hispanic or Latino ethnicity may be of any race; estimates for the race groups include Hispanics. Dash indicates data not available.
Source: U.S. Bureau of Labor Statistics.

Table 24. Median usual weekly earnings of full-time wage and salary workers 25 years and older, by educational attainment, 1979-2013 annual averages
[In current dollars]

Year	Total, 25 years and older	Less than a high school diploma	High school graduates, no college	Some college or associate degree	Bachelor's degree and higher
Total					
1979.........	$265	$210	$249	$282	$344
1980.........	286	222	266	304	376
1981.........	308	240	286	324	407
1982.........	327	248	302	351	438
1983.........	343	256	311	363	461
1984.........	362	263	323	382	486
1985.........	379	270	333	399	506
1986.........	391	278	344	409	525
1987.........	403	284	356	421	564
1988.........	414	288	368	430	585
1989.........	427	297	375	452	609
1990.........	449	303	386	476	638
1991.........	467	307	397	489	666
1992.........	479	311	403	484	696
1993.........	491	314	415	494	715
1994.........	500	307	421	499	733
1995.........	510	309	432	508	747
1996.........	520	317	443	518	758
1997.........	540	321	461	535	779
1998.........	572	337	479	558	821
1999.........	592	346	490	580	860
2000.........	609	362	505	596	891
2001.........	630	382	520	617	921
2002.........	646	388	535	629	941
2003.........	662	396	554	639	964
2004.........	683	401	574	661	986
2005.........	696	409	583	670	1,013
2006.........	718	419	595	692	1,039
2007.........	738	428	604	704	1,072
2008.........	761	453	618	722	1,115
2009.........	774	454	626	726	1,137
2010.........	782	444	626	734	1,144
2011.........	797	451	638	739	1,150
2012.........	815	471	652	749	1,165
2013.........	827	472	651	748	1,194
Women					
1979.........	$195	$152	$185	$211	$264
1980.........	213	164	201	231	290
1981.........	233	175	217	255	318
1982.........	255	184	236	274	346
1983.........	268	195	246	288	369
1984.........	283	200	259	305	390
1985.........	296	202	268	317	414
1986.........	308	208	277	330	436
1987.........	321	214	288	347	466
1988.........	335	221	298	360	485
1989.........	351	231	304	379	507
1990.........	369	240	315	395	535
1991.........	387	250	328	409	562
1992.........	400	256	337	407	594
1993.........	415	263	347	422	611
1994.........	421	257	351	423	634
1995.........	428	262	356	427	644
1996.........	444	268	365	442	657

Table 24. Median usual weekly earnings of full-time wage and salary workers 25 years and older, by educational attainment, 1979-2013 annual averages — Continued
[In current dollars]

Year	Total, 25 years and older	Less than a high school diploma	High school graduates, no college	Some college or associate degree	Bachelor's degree and higher
1997	462	275	378	459	672
1998	485	283	396	476	707
1999	497	290	405	488	740
2000	516	304	420	505	756
2001	543	316	443	520	786
2002	568	325	458	543	809
2003	584	329	474	560	832
2004	599	334	488	577	860
2005	612	341	493	587	883
2006	627	358	500	602	905
2007	646	369	512	609	932
2008	670	378	520	628	955
2009	687	382	542	630	970
2010	704	388	543	638	986
2011	718	395	554	645	998
2012	727	386	561	659	1,001
2013	740	400	573	657	1,043
Men					
1979	$314	$252	$308	$329	$396
1980	339	267	327	358	427
1981	372	286	356	389	475
1982	393	293	374	411	503
1983	407	301	388	422	518
1984	422	308	399	446	562
1985	443	314	407	472	590
1986	463	321	416	485	618
1987	477	324	423	497	653
1988	487	332	437	503	679
1989	500	346	450	517	705
1990	512	349	459	542	741
1991	523	349	470	563	764
1992	536	351	479	555	791
1993	555	356	487	572	806
1994	576	342	496	587	826
1995	588	347	507	596	845
1996	599	357	516	604	874
1997	615	365	535	621	896
1998	639	383	559	643	939
1999	668	395	580	665	977
2000	693	406	591	691	1,020
2001	720	419	609	723	1,067
2002	732	421	617	731	1,090
2003	744	429	628	740	1,131
2004	762	446	645	761	1,143
2005	771	455	652	766	1,167
2006	797	469	678	796	1,205
2007	823	481	689	810	1,243
2008	857	497	709	830	1,285
2009	873	500	716	835	1,327
2010	874	486	710	845	1,330
2011	886	488	720	840	1,332
2012	910	508	735	857	1,371
2013	912	500	732	858	1,395

Note: The comparability of historical labor force data has been affected at various times by methodological and other changes in the Current Population Survey (CPS). Information about historical comparability is online at www.bls.gov/cps/documentation.htm#comp.
Source: U.S. Bureau of Labor Statistics.

Table 25. Median hourly earnings of wage and salary workers paid hourly rates, by age, 1979-2013 annual averages

[In current dollars]

Year	Total, 16 years and older	16 to 24 years			25 years and older					
		Total	16 to 19 years	20 to 24 years	Total	25 to 34 years	35 to 44 years	45 to 54 years	55 to 64 years	65 years and older
Total										
1979.............	$4.44	$3.49	$3.10	$4.02	$5.11	$5.20	$5.29	$5.16	$4.97	$3.23
1980.............	4.82	3.71	3.22	4.29	5.55	5.66	5.76	5.65	5.39	3.56
1981.............	5.15	3.97	3.58	4.61	5.99	6.09	6.20	6.01	5.81	3.92
1982.............	5.40	4.05	3.60	4.66	6.28	6.35	6.61	6.42	6.11	4.12
1983.............	5.59	4.08	3.61	4.69	6.55	6.50	6.91	6.73	6.41	4.40
1984.............	5.83	4.18	3.65	4.82	6.84	6.77	7.17	7.08	6.62	4.63
1985.............	6.03	4.26	3.67	4.94	7.05	6.92	7.49	7.37	6.91	4.74
1986.............	6.20	4.41	3.71	5.06	7.23	7.01	7.79	7.73	7.17	4.97
1987.............	6.47	4.59	3.81	5.21	7.46	7.19	7.94	7.86	7.42	5.08
1988.............	6.73	4.79	4.03	5.38	7.74	7.43	8.17	8.16	7.48	5.23
1989.............	6.99	4.95	4.22	5.65	7.94	7.64	8.56	8.42	7.82	5.42
1990.............	7.23	5.16	4.49	5.91	8.16	7.90	8.82	8.79	8.02	5.75
1991.............	7.50	5.26	4.69	6.00	8.48	8.04	9.17	9.11	8.19	5.94
1992.............	7.72	5.37	4.73	6.03	8.73	8.17	9.38	9.52	8.48	6.14
1993.............	7.87	5.51	4.80	6.15	8.95	8.27	9.61	9.86	8.90	6.39
1994.............	8.01	5.62	4.91	6.22	9.12	8.38	9.92	10.02	9.02	6.39
1995.............	8.17	5.80	5.04	6.42	9.36	8.71	10.02	10.13	9.20	6.65
1996.............	8.40	5.94	5.17	6.69	9.62	8.82	10.14	10.24	9.39	6.77
1997.............	8.75	6.15	5.51	6.91	9.87	9.04	10.36	10.60	9.73	6.89
1998.............	9.10	6.58	5.88	7.24	10.13	9.65	10.86	10.96	10.08	7.40
1999.............	9.53	6.87	6.08	7.74	10.47	9.98	11.02	11.33	10.38	7.70
2000.............	9.91	7.24	6.41	8.07	10.88	10.18	11.35	11.82	10.82	8.05
2001.............	10.19	7.69	6.76	8.38	11.40	10.67	11.97	12.17	11.37	8.53
2002.............	10.47	7.81	6.91	8.47	11.83	10.98	12.18	12.46	11.85	9.07
2003.............	10.85	7.90	6.93	8.66	12.05	11.25	12.46	12.97	12.19	9.19
2004.............	11.00	7.98	7.00	8.78	12.23	11.37	12.89	13.23	12.58	9.62
2005.............	11.19	8.07	7.05	8.91	12.48	11.76	13.11	13.48	12.95	9.93
2006.............	11.76	8.24	7.23	9.16	12.94	11.95	13.49	14.03	13.33	10.15
2007.............	11.95	8.65	7.57	9.66	13.16	12.05	13.93	14.39	13.71	10.37
2008.............	12.23	8.87	7.84	9.76	13.81	12.50	14.38	14.87	14.20	10.89
2009.............	12.44	8.90	7.92	9.77	13.91	12.60	14.59	14.85	14.70	11.49
2010.............	12.50	8.90	8.00	9.53	13.98	12.53	14.61	14.98	14.89	11.55
2011.............	12.71	8.97	8.06	9.61	14.12	12.71	14.83	15.00	15.07	12.19
2012.............	12.80	9.05	8.10	9.70	14.25	12.82	14.86	15.07	15.39	12.21
2013.............	12.93	9.16	8.19	9.83	14.50	12.88	14.98	15.17	15.62	12.47
Women										
1979.............	$3.62	$3.19	$3.03	$3.52	$3.90	$4.04	$3.97	$3.84	$3.75	$3.12
1980.............	3.95	3.45	3.14	3.79	4.24	4.44	4.29	4.23	4.08	3.38
1981.............	4.28	3.71	3.52	4.09	4.69	4.89	4.77	4.59	4.43	3.71
1982.............	4.61	3.78	3.55	4.19	5.02	5.19	5.08	4.95	4.80	3.93
1983.............	4.80	3.82	3.55	4.26	5.23	5.44	5.31	5.19	5.07	4.16
1984.............	4.97	3.93	3.59	4.36	5.48	5.60	5.61	5.51	5.27	4.37
1985.............	5.13	4.01	3.61	4.56	5.73	5.79	5.91	5.76	5.46	4.43
1986.............	5.33	4.11	3.65	4.71	5.95	5.95	6.13	5.99	5.75	4.73
1987.............	5.60	4.22	3.71	4.89	6.16	6.14	6.35	6.28	6.03	4.85
1988.............	5.84	4.48	3.91	5.05	6.44	6.36	6.76	6.59	6.08	5.12
1989.............	6.11	4.69	4.10	5.23	6.78	6.68	7.10	6.90	6.38	5.14
1990.............	6.44	4.95	4.35	5.57	7.07	7.01	7.37	7.16	6.73	5.45
1991.............	6.75	5.08	4.64	5.71	7.34	7.19	7.73	7.61	6.95	5.76
1992.............	6.96	5.16	4.69	5.77	7.65	7.45	7.99	7.94	7.20	5.97
1993.............	7.12	5.27	4.73	5.96	7.87	7.61	8.16	8.18	7.56	6.18
1994.............	7.25	5.32	4.83	5.98	8.05	7.78	8.44	8.46	7.82	6.24
1995.............	7.46	5.49	4.94	6.09	8.17	7.92	8.63	8.72	7.93	6.45

Table 25. Median hourly earnings of wage and salary workers paid hourly rates, by age, 1979-2013 annual averages — Continued
[In current dollars]

Year	Total, 16 years and older	16 to 24 years			25 years and older					
		Total	16 to 19 years	20 to 24 years	Total	25 to 34 years	35 to 44 years	45 to 54 years	55 to 64 years	65 years and older
1996	7.73	5.68	5.09	6.26	8.43	8.06	8.89	8.94	8.07	6.45
1997	7.94	5.95	5.42	6.55	8.75	8.20	9.14	9.26	8.31	6.83
1998	8.23	6.24	5.78	6.93	9.13	8.80	9.66	9.78	8.85	7.21
1999	8.64	6.60	5.98	7.22	9.53	9.10	9.83	9.95	9.33	7.50
2000	9.06	7.00	6.23	7.80	9.89	9.69	10.03	10.18	9.84	7.87
2001	9.64	7.25	6.61	8.00	10.20	9.94	10.44	10.85	10.39	8.14
2002	9.89	7.45	6.80	8.11	10.71	10.12	10.98	11.18	10.81	8.73
2003	10.08	7.59	6.85	8.19	11.01	10.51	11.17	11.79	11.05	8.84
2004	10.17	7.71	6.86	8.32	11.23	10.62	11.45	11.95	11.57	9.16
2005	10.31	7.80	6.92	8.50	11.58	10.86	11.84	12.13	11.86	9.82
2006	10.65	7.99	7.11	8.82	11.87	11.07	12.05	12.26	12.12	9.97
2007	10.98	8.15	7.41	9.00	12.05	11.21	12.36	12.85	12.23	10.15
2008	11.49	8.43	7.71	9.16	12.48	11.72	12.89	13.16	13.00	10.53
2009	11.76	8.58	7.82	9.19	12.76	11.96	13.00	13.09	13.59	11.11
2010	11.83	8.62	7.91	9.08	12.88	12.04	13.12	13.50	13.68	11.18
2011	11.98	8.73	7.96	9.16	13.10	12.12	13.44	13.76	14.03	11.76
2012	11.99	8.78	8.02	9.17	13.17	12.15	13.46	13.80	14.36	11.84
2013	12.12	8.93	8.09	9.40	13.36	12.23	13.77	13.94	14.53	12.22
Men										
1979	$5.65	$3.90	$3.19	$4.64	$6.69	$6.38	$7.12	$7.10	$6.59	$3.56
1980	6.10	4.10	3.37	4.92	7.22	6.93	7.81	7.78	7.24	3.79
1981	6.57	4.31	3.64	5.11	7.78	7.33	8.30	8.49	7.88	4.21
1982	6.85	4.38	3.66	5.12	8.08	7.67	8.89	8.88	8.14	4.46
1983	6.92	4.38	3.67	5.05	8.31	7.74	9.22	9.16	8.74	4.75
1984	7.12	4.57	3.72	5.16	8.60	7.88	9.51	9.69	8.86	4.91
1985	7.33	4.68	3.75	5.23	8.85	8.00	9.80	9.97	9.04	4.99
1986	7.59	4.79	3.82	5.43	9.02	8.03	9.99	10.15	9.54	5.18
1987	7.77	4.91	3.95	5.68	9.16	8.26	10.10	10.24	9.72	5.32
1988	7.91	5.03	4.14	5.79	9.38	8.41	10.22	10.69	9.74	5.52
1989	8.10	5.17	4.39	6.02	9.71	8.56	10.59	10.88	10.00	5.90
1990	8.27	5.44	4.64	6.18	9.84	8.83	10.73	11.13	10.17	6.08
1991	8.59	5.58	4.74	6.23	9.98	8.94	10.98	11.71	10.08	6.22
1992	8.67	5.65	4.80	6.24	10.06	9.02	10.93	12.02	10.39	6.45
1993	8.86	5.75	4.87	6.33	10.18	9.10	11.16	12.15	10.96	6.71
1994	9.00	5.88	4.98	6.56	10.29	9.10	11.50	12.10	11.06	6.64
1995	9.23	6.04	5.14	6.82	10.73	9.46	11.89	12.32	11.11	6.85
1996	9.52	6.17	5.25	6.99	10.78	9.70	11.91	12.40	11.15	7.04
1997	9.83	6.45	5.61	7.18	11.10	9.92	12.07	12.80	11.79	6.96
1998	10.06	6.91	5.98	7.78	11.72	10.22	12.48	13.04	12.22	7.74
1999	10.31	7.12	6.18	8.03	12.00	10.84	12.78	13.68	12.21	7.86
2000	10.81	7.63	6.64	8.39	12.24	10.97	13.14	13.90	12.81	8.31
2001	11.32	8.01	6.90	8.92	12.88	11.58	13.92	14.25	12.95	9.00
2002	11.64	8.05	7.02	8.88	13.05	11.89	13.96	14.40	13.38	9.78
2003	11.89	8.14	7.02	9.00	13.25	12.01	14.13	14.93	14.09	9.79
2004	12.02	8.21	7.15	9.07	13.74	12.03	14.60	15.11	14.54	9.90
2005	12.16	8.42	7.21	9.20	13.91	12.17	14.88	15.13	14.79	10.04
2006	12.68	8.79	7.43	9.75	14.27	12.63	15.06	16.04	15.04	10.72
2007	12.95	9.13	7.77	9.96	14.75	12.83	15.17	16.15	15.45	11.01
2008	13.46	9.24	7.98	10.00	15.03	13.47	16.02	16.82	15.90	11.50
2009	13.76	9.22	8.05	9.99	15.07	13.20	16.10	16.99	16.09	12.00
2010	13.76	9.21	8.09	9.90	15.04	13.10	15.83	16.89	16.45	11.92
2011	13.80	9.23	8.16	9.90	15.11	13.18	16.03	16.88	17.07	12.85
2012	13.88	9.44	8.19	9.97	15.17	13.28	16.05	16.99	17.28	13.03
2013	14.00	9.67	8.37	10.00	15.27	13.42	16.21	17.17	17.28	12.88

Note: The comparability of historical labor force data has been affected at various times by methodological and other changes in the Current

Population Survey (CPS). Information about historical comparability is online at www.bls.gov/cps/documentation.htm#comp.
Source: U.S. Bureau of Labor Statistics.

Table 26. Median hourly earnings of wage and salary workers paid hourly rates, by race and Hispanic or Latino ethnicity, 1979-2013 annual averages
[In current dollars]

Year	Total, 16 years and older	White	Black or African American	Asian	Hispanic or Latino ethnicity
Total					
1979	$4.44	$4.51	$4.11	–	$4.08
1980	4.82	4.88	4.44	–	4.44
1981	5.15	5.18	4.90	–	4.81
1982	5.40	5.47	5.06	–	5.01
1983	5.59	5.66	5.15	–	5.09
1984	5.83	5.90	5.36	–	5.27
1985	6.03	6.10	5.50	–	5.47
1986	6.20	6.28	5.80	–	5.65
1987	6.47	6.56	5.99	–	5.82
1988	6.73	6.81	6.15	–	5.95
1989	6.99	7.08	6.43	–	6.07
1990	7.23	7.33	6.81	–	6.28
1991	7.50	7.61	7.00	–	6.46
1992	7.72	7.82	7.06	–	6.65
1993	7.87	7.97	7.18	–	6.83
1994	8.01	8.11	7.29	–	6.93
1995	8.17	8.32	7.66	–	7.00
1996	8.40	8.57	7.76	–	7.17
1997	8.75	8.88	8.01	–	7.39
1998	9.10	9.22	8.39	–	7.92
1999	9.53	9.74	8.85	–	8.07
2000	9.91	9.96	9.34	$10.07	8.54
2001	10.19	10.26	9.78	10.75	9.06
2002	10.47	10.71	9.93	10.36	9.22
2003	10.85	10.97	10.15	11.12	9.76
2004	11.00	11.13	10.19	11.10	9.81
2005	11.19	11.48	10.17	12.01	9.95
2006	11.76	11.86	10.66	12.53	10.12
2007	11.95	12.08	10.89	12.22	10.24
2008	12.23	12.54	11.20	13.01	10.97
2009	12.44	12.66	11.64	13.16	11.04
2010	12.50	12.74	11.77	13.22	10.88
2011	12.71	12.91	11.79	13.35	11.05
2012	12.80	13.04	11.84	13.23	11.12
2013	12.93	13.15	11.90	13.62	11.25
Women					
1979	$3.62	$3.62	$3.55	–	$3.44
1980	3.95	3.96	3.88	–	3.78
1981	4.28	4.28	4.19	–	4.10
1982	4.61	4.61	4.49	–	4.33
1983	4.80	4.81	4.72	–	4.42
1984	4.97	4.98	4.87	–	4.65
1985	5.13	5.14	5.04	–	4.82
1986	5.33	5.35	5.17	–	5.00
1987	5.60	5.62	5.40	–	5.11
1988	5.84	5.86	5.61	–	5.28
1989	6.11	6.13	5.88	–	5.53
1990	6.44	6.46	6.23	–	5.80
1991	6.75	6.76	6.55	–	5.98
1992	6.96	6.99	6.64	–	6.17
1993	7.12	7.16	6.87	–	6.31
1994	7.25	7.34	6.93	–	6.40
1995	7.46	7.54	7.12	–	6.60
1996	7.73	7.79	7.20	–	6.77

Table 26. Median hourly earnings of wage and salary workers paid hourly rates, by race and Hispanic or Latino ethnicity, 1979-2013 annual averages — Continued
[In current dollars]

Year	Total, 16 years and older	White	Black or African American	Asian	Hispanic or Latino ethnicity
1997	7.94	8.00	7.59	–	6.82
1998	8.23	8.33	7.90	–	7.22
1999	8.64	8.73	8.13	–	7.46
2000	9.06	9.09	8.86	$9.77	7.89
2001	9.64	9.73	9.15	10.07	8.28
2002	9.89	9.94	9.45	10.10	8.54
2003	10.08	10.11	9.91	10.68	8.88
2004	10.17	10.21	9.93	10.57	9.04
2005	10.31	10.50	9.93	11.64	9.18
2006	10.65	10.77	10.11	11.95	9.50
2007	10.98	11.06	10.45	11.83	9.80
2008	11.49	11.70	10.78	12.25	10.07
2009	11.76	11.83	11.01	12.67	10.09
2010	11.83	11.88	11.20	12.41	10.11
2011	11.98	12.05	11.28	12.80	10.25
2012	11.99	12.08	11.23	12.75	10.21
2013	12.12	12.21	11.54	13.04	10.49
Men					
1979	$5.65	$5.79	$4.89	–	$4.79
1980	6.10	6.23	5.18	–	5.03
1981	6.57	6.71	5.81	–	5.37
1982	6.85	6.98	5.97	–	5.73
1983	6.92	7.07	5.96	–	5.81
1984	7.12	7.26	6.16	–	6.04
1985	7.33	7.58	6.15	–	6.07
1986	7.59	7.78	6.57	–	6.19
1987	7.77	7.93	6.74	–	6.37
1988	7.91	8.06	6.94	–	6.51
1989	8.10	8.28	7.07	–	6.66
1990	8.27	8.55	7.37	–	6.74
1991	8.59	8.82	7.57	–	6.88
1992	8.67	8.89	7.62	–	6.99
1993	8.86	9.07	7.67	–	7.12
1994	9.00	9.21	7.92	–	7.17
1995	9.23	9.62	8.16	–	7.26
1996	9.52	9.79	8.18	–	7.62
1997	9.83	9.96	8.67	–	7.90
1998	10.06	10.18	9.09	–	8.24
1999	10.31	10.61	9.77	–	8.61
2000	10.81	10.95	9.98	$10.79	9.04
2001	11.32	11.61	10.18	11.84	9.67
2002	11.64	11.86	10.24	11.02	9.92
2003	11.89	12.03	10.81	11.89	10.03
2004	12.02	12.16	10.88	11.90	10.02
2005	12.16	12.47	10.90	12.75	10.19
2006	12.68	12.88	11.42	13.18	10.84
2007	12.95	13.22	11.57	13.22	11.07
2008	13.46	13.85	11.99	14.03	11.83
2009	13.76	13.95	12.27	14.01	11.92
2010	13.76	13.97	12.16	14.11	11.73
2011	13.80	14.02	12.06	14.25	11.81
2012	13.88	14.17	12.20	14.15	11.96
2013	14.00	14.24	12.16	14.24	11.99

Note: The comparability of historical labor force data has been affected at various times by methodological and other changes in the Current Population Survey (CPS). Information about historical comparability is online at www.bls.gov/cps/documentation.htm#comp. As of 2003, estimates for the race groups shown (White, Black or African American, and Asian) include people who selected that race group only; people who selected more

67

than one race group are not included. Prior to 2003, people who reported more than one race were included in the group they identified as the main race. Asian data for 2000-2002 are for Asians and Pacific Islanders. As of 2003, Asians constitute a separate category. Data for Asians were not tabulated prior to 2000. People of Hispanic or Latino ethnicity may be of any race; estimates for the race groups include Hispanics. Dash indicates data not available.
Source: U.S. Bureau of Labor Statistics.

Technical Notes

The estimates in this report were obtained from the Current Population Survey (CPS), which provides information on the labor force, employment, and unemployment. The survey is conducted monthly for the U.S. Bureau of Labor Statistics (BLS) by the U.S. Census Bureau using a scientifically selected national sample of about 60,000 eligible households representing all 50 states and the District of Columbia. The survey also provides data on earnings, which are based on one-fourth of the CPS monthly sample and are limited to wage and salary workers. All self-employed workers, both incorporated and unincorporated, are excluded from the data presented in this report.

It is important to note that the comparisons of earnings in this report are on a broad level and do not control for many factors that can be significant in explaining earnings differences. This includes the direct comparisons of earnings levels among demographic groups discussed in the narrative and the women's-to-men's earnings ratios shown in the tables (that is, women's earnings as a percentage of men's). For example, the overall ratio of women's-to-men's earnings for full-time workers presented here is not controlled for differences in important determinants of earnings such as age, occupation, and educational attainment. Readers should not construe the earnings comparisons in this report as being restricted to workers with otherwise comparable characteristics and comparable jobs. One must be cautious even when attempting to control for one of the important factors that may explain earnings differences. Comparisons of women's and men's earnings by detailed occupation, for example, are not simultaneously controlled for differences in key factors such as job skills and responsibilities, work experience, and specialization.

Material in this report is in the public domain and may be used without permission. This information is available to sensory-impaired individuals upon request. Voice telephone: (202) 691-5200; Federal Relay Service: 1 (800) 877-8339.

Concepts and definitions

The principal concepts and definitions used in connection with the earnings data in this report are described briefly below.

Wage and salary workers. These are workers age 16 and older who receive wages, salaries, commissions, tips, payments in kind, or piece rates on their sole or principal job. This group includes employees in both the public and private sectors. All self-employed workers are excluded whether or not their businesses are incorporated.

Full-time workers. People who usually work 35 hours or more per week at their sole or principal job are defined as working full time for the purpose of these estimates. The federal Fair Labor Standards Act (FLSA) does not define full- or part-time employment.

Part-time workers. People who usually work fewer than 35 hours per week at their sole or principal job are defined as working part time for the purpose of these estimates. The federal Fair Labor Standards Act (FLSA) does not define full- or part-time employment.

Usual weekly earnings. The data represent earnings before taxes and other deductions and include any overtime pay, commissions, or tips usually received (at the main job in the case of multiple jobholders). Prior to 1994, respondents were asked how much they usually earned per week. Since January 1994, respondents have been asked to identify the easiest way for them to report earnings (hourly, weekly, biweekly, twice monthly, monthly, annually, or other) and how much they usually earn in the reported time period. Earnings reported on a basis other than weekly are converted to a weekly equivalent. The term "usual" is determined by each respondent's own understanding of the term. If the respondent asks for a definition of "usual," interviewers are instructed to define the term as more than half the weeks worked during the past 4 or 5 months.

Medians of usual weekly earnings. The earnings estimates shown in this report are medians. The median is the midpoint in a given earnings distribution, with half of workers having earnings above the median and the other half having earnings below the median.

The BLS procedure for estimating the median of a weekly earnings distribution places each reported or calculated weekly earnings value into a $50-wide interval that is centered around a multiple of $50. The median is calculated through the linear interpolation of the interval in which the median lies.

Changes over time in the medians for specific groups may not necessarily be consistent with the movements estimated for the overall median boundary. The most common reasons for this possible anomaly are as follows:

- There could be a change in the relative weights of the subgroups. For example, the median earnings of 16- to 24-year-olds and the median earnings of those 25 years and older may rise, but if the lower earning 16-to-24 age group accounts for a greatly increased share of the total, the overall median could actually fall.

- There could be a large change in the shape of the distribution of reported earnings, particularly near a median boundary. This change could be caused by survey observations that are clustered at rounded values, such as $600 or $700. An estimate lying in a $50-wide centered interval containing such a cluster tends to change more slowly than one in other intervals. Consider, for example, the calculation of the median for a multipeaked earnings distribution that shifts over time. As such a distribution shifts, the median does not necessarily move at the same rate. Specifically, the median takes relatively more time to move through a frequently reported earnings interval, but once above the upper limit of such an interval, it can move relatively quickly to the next frequently reported interval. BLS procedures for estimating medians mitigate such irregular movements; however, users should be cautious of these effects when evaluating short-term changes in the medians and in ratios of the medians.

Workers paid by the hour. These are employed wage and salary workers who report that they are paid at an hourly rate on their job. Typically, workers paid an hourly wage have made up approximately three-fifths of all wage and salary workers. Estimates of workers paid by the hour include both full- and part-time workers unless otherwise specified.

Hourly earnings. These data are for wage and salary workers who are paid by the hour and pertain to earnings from a person's sole or principal job. Hourly earnings for hourly paid workers do not include overtime pay, commissions, or tips received.

Workers paid at or below the federal minimum wage. The CPS does not include questions on whether workers are covered by the minimum wage provisions of the federal Fair Labor Standards Act (FLSA) or by individual state or local minimum wage laws. The estimates of workers paid at or below the federal minimum wage in this report are based solely on whether the hourly wage they report (which does not include overtime pay, tips, or commissions) is at or below the federal minimum wage. It should be noted that some respondents might round hourly earnings when answering survey questions. As a result, some workers might be reported as having hourly earnings above or below the federal minimum wage when in fact they earn the minimum wage.

Some workers reported as earning at or below the prevailing federal minimum wage may not in fact be covered by federal or state minimum wage laws because of exclusions and exemptions in the statutes. Thus, the presence of workers with hourly earnings below the federal minimum wage does not necessarily indicate violations of the FLSA or state statutes in cases where such standards apply.

The estimates of the number of workers with reported earnings at or below the federal minimum wage pertain only to workers who are paid hourly rates. Salaried workers and other nonhourly paid workers are excluded, even though some have earnings that, if converted to hourly rates, would be at or below the federal minimum wage. Consequently, the estimates presented in this report likely understate the actual number of workers with hourly earnings at or below the minimum wage. BLS does not routinely estimate the hourly earnings of workers not paid by the hour because there are data quality concerns associated with constructing such an estimate.

Regular collection of earnings data in the basic CPS began in 1979. The prevailing federal minimum wage for 1979 and later years is listed below.

Federal minimum wage	Effective date
$2.90	January 1, 1979
$3.10	January 1, 1980
$3.35	January 1, 1981
$3.80	April 1, 1990
$4.25	April 1, 1991
$4.75	October 1, 1996
$5.15	September 1, 1997
$5.85	July 24, 2007
$6.55	July 24, 2008
$7.25	July 24, 2009

When the minimum wage has increased during a given year, the estimates of the annual average number of minimum wage workers reflect both minimum wage levels in effect during the year. For example, data for 2007 reflect the number of workers who earned the federal minimum wage of $5.15 for January to July and the number of workers who earned the minimum wage of $5.85 for August to December.

Race. In the survey process, race is determined by the household respondent. In accordance with the Office of Management and Budget guidelines, White, Black or African American, and Asian are terms used to describe a person's race. Beginning in 2003, people in these categories are those who selected that race group only. Those who identify multiple race groups are categorized as people of two or more races. Prior to 2003, people of two or more races identified one group as their main race. More information on the 2003 changes to questions on race is available at **http://www.bls.gov/cps/rvcps03.pdf**. Data for other race groups—American Indians and Alaska Natives, Native Hawaiians and Other Pacific Islanders—and for people of two or more races are included in totals but not separately identified in this report because the number of survey respondents is too small to develop estimates of sufficient quality.

Hispanic or Latino ethnicity. This phrase refers to people who identified themselves in the survey process as being of Hispanic, Latino, or Spanish origin. People whose ethnicity is identified as Hispanic or Latino may be of any race and are included in estimates for the race groups (White, Black or African American, and Asian) in addition to being shown separately.

Inflation adjustment/constant dollars. The Consumer Price Index research series using current methods (CPI-U-RS) is used to convert current dollars to constant dollars for the inflation-adjusted median earnings estimates shown in this report. BLS has made numerous improvements to the Consumer Price Index (CPI) over the years. Although these improvements make the CPI more accurate, the official histories of price index series are not adjusted to reflect the improvements. Because many researchers need a historical series that measures price change consistently over time, BLS developed the CPI-U-RS to provide an estimate of the CPI that incorporates most of the methodological improvements made since 1978 into the entire series. For further information, see Kenneth J. Stewart and Stephen B. Reed, "CPI research series using current methods, 1978–98," Monthly Labor Review, June 1999, available at **http://www.bls.gov/opub/mlr/1999/06/cpimlr.pdf**; and "Questions and Answers: Consumer Price Index Research Series Using Current Methods," at **http://www.bls.gov/cpi/cpirsqa.pdf**.

This report uses the most recent version of the CPI-U-RS available at the time of production. Users should note that the CPI-U-RS is subject to periodic revision. As a result, the rate of inflation incorporated into the inflation-adjusted median earnings estimates in this report may differ from the rate used in previous reports in this series or in other publications.

Reliability

Statistics based on the CPS are subject to both sampling and nonsampling error. When a sample, rather than the entire population, is surveyed, there is a chance that the sample estimates may differ from the true population values they represent. The component of this difference that occurs because samples differ by chance is known as sampling error, and its variability is measured by the standard error of the estimate. There is about a 90-percent chance, or level of confidence, that an estimate based on a sample will differ by no more than 1.6 standard errors from the true population value because of sampling error. BLS analyses are generally conducted at the 90-percent level of confidence.

The CPS data also are affected by nonsampling error. Nonsampling error can occur for many reasons, including the failure to sample a segment of the population, inability to obtain information on all respondents in the sample, inability or unwillingness of respondents to provide correct information, and errors made in the collection or processing of the data.

Information about the reliability of data from the CPS is available at **http://ww.bls.gov/cps/documentation.htm#reliability**.